Oxford School Shakespeare

Macbeth

edited by

Roma Gill, OBE
M.A. *Cantab*. B.Litt. *Oxon*.

Oxford University Press

OXFORD
UNIVERSITY PRESS

Great Clarendon Street, Oxford OX2 6DP

Oxford University Press is a department of the University of Oxford.
It furthers the University's objective of excellence in research, scholarship,
and education by publishing worldwide in

Oxford New York

Athens Auckland Bangkok Bogotá Buenos Aires Calcutta
Cape Town Chennai Dar es Salaam Delhi Florence Hong Kong Istanbul
Karachi Kuala Lumpur Madrid Melbourne Mexico City Mumbai
Nairobi Paris São Paulo Singapore Taipei Tokyo Toronto Warsaw
with associated companies in Berlin Ibadan

Oxford is a registered trade mark of Oxford University Press
in the UK and in certain other countries

© Oxford University Press 1977
First published 1977
Reprinted 1978, 1980, 1981 (twice), 1982, 1983, 1984 (twice),1985,
1986 (twice), 1987, 1988, 1989, 1990, 1991, 1992
Revised edition first published 1992
Reprinted 1992, 1993 (twice), 1994 (twice), 1995 (twice), 1996,
1997, (twice), 1998 (twice), 1999 (twice)
Trade edition first published 1994
Reprinted 1994, 1995, 1996, 1997 (twice), 1998 (twice), 1999

ISBN 0 19 831981 9 (Trade edition) 10
ISBN 0 19 831970 3 (School edition) 17 19 20 18 16

Illustrations by Coral Mula

Cover photograph by Reg Wilson shows Albert Finney as Macbeth in
the National Theatre's 1978 production of *Macbeth*.

For Mandy

Oxford School Shakespeare
edited by Roma Gill

A Midsummer Night's Dream	Twelfth Night
Romeo and Juliet	The Taming of the Shrew
As You Like It	Othello
Macbeth	Hamlet
Julius Caesar	King Lear
The Merchant of Venice	Henry V
Henry IV Part I	The Winter's Tale
Antony and Cleopatra	The Tempest

Printed in the United Kingdom at the University Press, Cambridge

Contents

Macbeth: A play for the king

When Elizabeth I of England was dying, childless, she named James VI of Scotland as her successor. He became James I of England.

In August 1606 James was at Hampton Court, a palace near London, entertaining his brother-in-law, King Christian of Denmark. A play was acted for them, *Macbeth*, written by the best dramatist of the time, William Shakespeare. It was a new play, but the story was an old one. James knew it well, because it was about ancestors, Banquo and Fleance, through whom he had inherited the throne of Scotland.

Shakespeare found the story in *The History of Scotland*, by Raphael Holinshed, but his play is much more than a dramatic re-writing of the historical facts. He made many changes, and the biggest of these concerned James's ancestor. In the true story, Banquo joined Macbeth in killing Duncan; but clearly it would be tactless to suggest that James was descended from a regicide—the murderer of a king. So Shakespeare's Banquo is innocent.

James also believed that he was descended spiritually from the long tradition of English monarchs, and that he had inherited the power of healing that Edward the Confessor (1042–66) possessed. Shakespeare's description of this power (*4*, 3, 146–56) is, to some extent, deliberate flattery of his king. Shakespeare also knew that James was extremely interested in witchcraft, and had written a book about it.

Macbeth is certainly a play 'fit for a king'.

But of course it is more than this—more than flattery for an ancient British monarch; and although the story is largely true, we do not read *Macbeth* as 'history'. We could interpret Shakespeare's play as a moral lesson. Macbeth murders his king. To murder any man is a crime, but those who lived at the time of Shakespeare thought that the murder of a *king* was the greatest of all crimes. Kings were appointed by God, to rule as His deputies: rebellion against a true king was rebellion against God. By murdering Duncan, Macbeth gains the crown; but he loses love, friendship, respect—and in the end his life. His crime is rightly punished.

There is still more to the play. On one 'level' it is royal entertainment—and entertainment, too, for all those of us who

enjoy the suspense and excitement of a murder story. On another
level, it teaches us, in a new way, the old lesson that crime does not
pay. But there are two more levels.

As we look at the character of Macbeth we see, more clearly
than we are able to see in real life, the effects of uncontrolled
ambition on a man who is, except for his ambition, noble in nature.
Macbeth has full knowledge of right and wrong; he knows that
he has committed a very great crime by murdering Duncan.
Shakespeare shows us how Macbeth becomes hardened to his
crimes, and yet how he suffers from fears which he has created
himself.

On the last level, the play has great power as a work of poetry
and imagination. The language is rich in sound and meaning, full
of pictures, and immensely varied. Take this episode, for example.
When Macbeth comes from the murder of Duncan, his hands are
covered in the king's blood; he looks at them, and feels that all the
waters in the ocean cannot wash away the blood, but that

> this my hand will rather
> The multitudinous seas incarnadine,
> Making the green one red.   (2, 2, 61–3)

The word 'multitudinous' gives a sense of vastness, and
'incarnadine' (meaning 'redden') is another impressive word;
its length and sound give strength to the meaning. The two words
are more Latin than English, and were very new to the English
language; Shakespeare was one of the first writers to use them.
They are followed by the simplest, most direct words. Imagine
a film camera. First the camera shows you a picture of endless
waters, stretching as far as the eye can see: then a sudden close-up
picture, perhaps a small pool of green water that turns red with
blood as we look at it. Such skill in the use of language is unique.

Although I have distinguished four levels on which the play
Macbeth can work, I do not want to give the impression that these
levels can in fact be separated from each other. The entertainment,
the moral teaching, the psychology, and the poetry are often all
contained in the same speech—even, sometimes, in the same line.
Macbeth demands an alert reader.

No summary can do justice to the play. At best, a commentary
such as this can be no more than a map. It can show the roads, and
even point out the important places; but it is no substitute for
reading the play.

Leading characters in the play

Duncan The king of Scotland, murdered by Macbeth. Duncan is a true and gracious king, who represents the Elizabethan concept that the king was appointed by God, and is therefore almost divine.

Malcolm Duncan's elder son. Early in the play Malcolm is named as the next king of Scotland. After Duncan's murder Malcolm, with his brother Donalbain, escapes from Scotland. He takes refuge in England, at the court of Edward the Confessor, until he is able to lead an army against Macbeth. At the end of the play he is crowned king of Scotland.

Macbeth A mighty and ambitious warrior, one of the leaders of Duncan's army. He hears a prophecy that he will be king one day. This makes him more ambitious and leads him to murder Duncan. He is elected king of Scotland, but he becomes a cruel and unjust ruler. He is always conscious of guilt, and never knows a moment's peace after he has killed Duncan. At the end of the play he is killed by Macduff. (See also p. xix.)

Lady Macbeth She is even more ambitious than her husband, and has no regard for morality. She urges Macbeth to kill Duncan, and refuses to understand his doubts and hesitations. Husband and wife are at first affectionate, hiding nothing from each other; gradually this relationship is destroyed. Lady Macbeth becomes obsessed with the murder of Duncan, suffers from nightmares, and finally kills herself.

Banquo He and Macbeth are the leaders of Duncan's army, but he is not so conspicuously valiant as Macbeth. It is prophesied that his children will be kings, but although he hopes that this prophecy will come true, he takes no action. He is killed by murderers working for Macbeth, but his son, Fleance, escapes.

Macduff A Scottish thane (nobleman), who comes to prominence after the murder of Duncan. Macbeth is particularly afraid of him, and orders murderers to kill Lady Macduff and her children. Macduff persuades Malcolm to lead an army against Macbeth, and it is he who kills Macbeth.

Ross ⎡Although Ross has a large part in the play, he does not really have
⎢a 'character'. He brings messages, describes events, warns of
⎣dangers to come, and comments on the progress of the play.

Macbeth: The play

Act 1

Scene 1   A very short scene opens the play. It is long enough to awaken curiosity, but not to satisfy it. We have come in at the *end* of the witches' meeting, just as they are arranging their next appointment before their 'familiar spirits'—devils in animal shapes—call them away into the 'fog and filthy air'. The mood of the play is set here, although the action does not start until the next scene. Here we

Scene 2 learn about the tough battle, about the rebels who seem to have all the luck, and about two brave men, Macbeth and Banquo, who win the victory for Scotland. Duncan rewards Macbeth for his courage by giving him the title 'thane of Cawdor'; but we ought to remember that the title first belonged to one who was 'a most disloyal traitor'.

Scene 3 The witches' malice and magic are shown, as they await Macbeth on the lonely moor (a wasteland area). They have power over the winds, and can make life miserable for such men as the captain of the ship, 'The Tiger'. Their dance, when they hear Macbeth's drum, is made up of steps in groups of three— the magical number. Macbeth and Banquo, however, are ordinary human beings, tired after the day's fighting and grumbling about the weather. Banquo is almost amused by the witches; he cannot bring himself to think of them as women because 'your beards forbid me to interpret / That you are so'. Macbeth is stunned to silence by their prophecies, but Banquo questions them calmly.

  The audience can judge the witches better than Macbeth can; *we* know, from the previous scene, that his courage, and not the witches' magic, has won him the title 'thane of Cawdor'; and we are not surprised, as he is, when Ross calls him by this title. While Ross, Angus, and Banquo speak together (perhaps at the back of the stage), Macbeth speaks his own thoughts aloud in a soliloquy— a speech not intended by the speaker to be overheard. They are frightening thoughts: they frighten Macbeth as well as us, for murder is in his mind. He tries to reject this first impulse, declaring that he will leave everything to chance:

> If chance will have me king, why, chance may crown me
> Without my stir.

Scene 4   When Duncan hears of the death of the treacherous thane of Cawdor, he utters a very meaningful remark:

> There's no art
> To find the mind's construction in the face.
> He was a gentleman on whom I built
> An absolute trust.

We have not seen the traitor, so we do not know how appropriate these words are for *him*; but we have seen his successor, and Macbeth is certainly a gentleman on whom Duncan is building 'An absolute trust'. Duncan's comment could also be applied to other persons and happenings in this play, where things are not what they seem to be, where 'Fair is foul and foul is fair'.
Duncan now makes a very important announcement:

> We will establish our estate upon
> Our eldest, Malcolm, whom we name hereafter
> The Prince of Cumberland.

In the time of Duncan the crown of Scotland was not passed automatically from father to son. Instead, the king could name his successor, as Duncan does here, and grant him the title 'Prince of Cumberland'. If the king were to die without naming an heir, or if the heir was not acceptable, the Scottish nobles could elect a new king. We hear that Macbeth is thus elected in *Act 2*, Scene 4. Duncan's choice comes as a great shock to Macbeth, for he recognizes it as an obstacle standing between him and the crown. At the end of the scene he admits to possessing 'black and deep desires', but he is afraid to speak these openly, even to himself.

Scene 5   We already know the contents of Macbeth's letter to his wife; but the letter is important because it shows us something of the relationship between Macbeth and Lady Macbeth: he has no secrets from her, and she is his 'dearest partner of greatness'. Lady Macbeth understands her husband well. She knows that he has great ambitions, but she also knows that he is honourable, and that this sense of honour will not allow him to 'catch the nearest way'. She knows that she will have to urge her husband on to become

king, and she calls for evil spirits to help her. She will give up all the
gentle, tender qualities of a woman, so that she can become a sexless,
pitiless fiend. She takes full control over the situation, and Macbeth
seems glad to let her have the responsibility.

Scene 7   Alone after dinner, Macbeth has the opportunity to think
about the murder of his king, perhaps for the first time. At first
murder had been only a dream, 'but fantastical' (*I*, 3, 139), but
now it is a real moral problem. He knows that the crime must be
punished; divine justice in a 'life to come' does not worry him so
much as judgement in this earthly life. Then he considers the duties
he owes to Duncan—the duties of a kinsman, of a subject to his
king, and of a host to his guest. Finally he thinks of the character
of Duncan, a king of almost divine excellence.

Macbeth has a vision of the heavenly powers, horrified by
this murder; he sees Pity, personified as a 'naked new-born babe'
which is nevertheless 'Striding the blast', while 'heaven's cherubin'
are mounted on the winds. The speech builds to a mighty climax—
then suddenly the power is lost, when Macbeth turns to his own
wretched motive for committing such a crime. He can find nothing
except 'Vaulting ambition', and even now he realizes that too high
a leap ('vault') can only lead to a fall.

His mind is made up, and he tells his wife 'We will proceed no
further in this business'. He is not prepared for her rage and abuse.
She calls him a coward, insults his virility, and declares that she
would have murdered her child while it was feeding at her breast,
rather than break such a promise as Macbeth has done. Defeated
by his wife's scorn, and persuaded by her encouragement, Macbeth
agrees to murder his king. —whipped

Act 2

Scene 1   The witches have disturbed Banquo, as well as Macbeth. As he
crosses the courtyard of Macbeth's castle he hears a noise, and calls
for his sword: this suggests tension, for he should not need a sword
in a friend's home. Macbeth also shows signs of stress, for he speaks
few words in his replies to Banquo; and when he is alone, the strain
shows very clearly. He is living in a nightmare, but although he is
at first alarmed by the dagger that his imagination creates, he seems

later to *enjoy* the horror of the moment. The last lines of the scene
could even show a grim humour:

> the bell invites me.
> Hear it not, Duncan; for it is a knell
> That summons thee to heaven, or to hell.

Scene 2   Lady Macbeth is as tense as her husband, and she has been drinking to give herself courage. Her speech is jerky, for she reacts to
every sound, and when her husband comes from the king's room,
his hands red with Duncan's blood, she greets him with relief and
pride: 'My husband'. He has now proved himself, in her eyes, to
be a man. Macbeth slowly awakens from the nightmare he has
been living in and realizes what a terrible crime he has committed.
He speaks of the real sounds he has heard, and then of the voice
that cried

> 'Sleep no more!
> Macbeth does murder sleep'

This ban will be carried out: never again will Macbeth, or his wife,
have any rest, and from time to time throughout the play they will
comment on their weariness and lack of refreshing sleep.

For the present, however, Lady Macbeth again takes charge
of the situation. Early in this scene she revealed some natural,
womanly feelings when she confessed that she could not murder
Duncan herself because he 'resembled / My father as he slept'.
But now she speaks a line which shows, terrifyingly, how little she
thinks of the guilt that she shares with her husband:

> A little water clears us of this deed.

Scene 3   The mood of the play suddenly changes. The audience has
been as tense as Macbeth and Lady Macbeth in the last scene, and
we need to relax a little now. The Porter, woken from a drunken
sleep, gives us something to laugh at. His jokes are not so funny
today as they were in 1606, when his chatter about the 'equivocator'
might have reminded the audience of the recent and notorious
trial of a priest who could 'swear in both the scales against either
scale'; but the wise observations on drink and lechery are still
amusing.

Macduff and Lennox come almost from another world; or
perhaps the Porter is more accurate than he thinks when he
pretends to be porter at the gate of hell. The tension mounts again
as we wait for the murder to be discovered.

Lennox's description of the 'unruly' night would have been full of significance to the Elizabethans. They firmly believed that any disorder in human affairs was reflected by disorder in the world of nature. Macbeth is cautious, but we cannot miss the understatement of his reply to Lennox: ''twas a rough night'.

The moment we have been waiting for arrives. Macduff's words emphasize the fact that this is more than an ordinary murder:

> Confusion now has made his masterpiece!
> Most sacrilegious murder hath broke ope
> The Lord's anointed temple.

The scene is chaotic: alarm-bells ring, and characters appear from all sides of the stage. Macduff is almost hysterical; the king's sons are afraid; Macbeth impulsively kills Duncan's servants—and by doing so arouses Macduff's suspicion. The speech in which Macbeth attempts to justify himself may perhaps convince the other thanes; but we know how false it is, and the elaborate images (for example, 'His silver skin lac'd with his golden blood') stress this falsehood. Lady Macbeth knows the truth too, for she faints (or pretends to faint) and some attention is drawn away from her husband.

Scene 4   The short scene between Ross and the Old Man serves three purposes. At first it continues the comparison begun in Lennox's lines in Scene 3 between the human world and the natural world, mentioning strange events and stressing that they are

> unnatural,
> Even like the deed that's done.

The second function of the scene appears when Macduff enters to bring more news: it indicates the passing of time. Thirdly, it brings Macduff into greater prominence, because it allows the actor playing the part of Macduff to reveal, by the tone of his voice, that Macduff continues to be suspicious of Macbeth, and that he does not himself believe the answers he gives to Ross's questions.

Act 3

Scene 1   Banquo also is suspicious of Macbeth:

> Thou hast it now: King, Cawdor, Glamis, all,
> As the weird women promis'd; and, I fear,
> Thou play'dst most foully for 't.

But he thinks about the prophecy concerning his own children, and this gives him hope. Macbeth too has been thinking about this prophecy, and it gives him cause for bitterness: he realizes that his crown is 'fruitless', and his sceptre 'barren' (see illustration, p. 65). He murdered Duncan in order to make the witches' prophecy come true, but now he plots to murder Banquo and Fleance so that the witches' promise to Banquo may *not* come true.

Scene 2   Lady Macbeth now begins to show signs of strain, and we hear that Macbeth suffers 'terrible dreams'. For a moment Macbeth and his wife show understanding and sympathy for each other, but the moment does not last long. Macbeth keeps secret from his wife the plot to murder Banquo. He alarms her by conjuring up an atmosphere of evil, and once again he appears to enjoy his dreadful imaginings (just as he did when he went to murder Duncan). But it is a mistake to hide the facts from Lady Macbeth: this is the beginning of the break in their relationship.

When Macbeth calls upon 'seeling night' to hide his wickedness, we remember how Lady Macbeth, before the murder of Duncan, had called for the night, shrouded in 'the dunnest smoke of hell' (*1*, 5, 50), to hide the murdering dagger from the sight of heaven.

Scene 3   Outside the castle, the two murderers wait for Banquo and Fleance. It is a surprise, to us as well as to them, when a third hired assassin appears. Macbeth can trust no-one, not even the thugs he first appointed to murder Banquo.

Scene 4   The confusion of Banquo's murder contrasts well with the ceremony of the state banquet. The formality is announced in the first line: 'You know your own degrees; sit down'; and the scene proceeds with dignity for some time. The appearance of one of Banquo's murderers disturbs the peace for Macbeth. The state occasion demands courteous behaviour from the king, but when the murderer says that Fleance has escaped, Macbeth is agitated. Banquo's Ghost, which only Macbeth can see, adds to this distress, until the whole scene breaks into fragments, and Lady Macbeth has to ask her guests to leave, without any of the formality with which they arrived:

> Stand not upon the order of your going,
> But go at once.

The banquet is symbolic as well as realistic, and Shakespeare is careful that we do not overlook this aspect. As soon as the guests are seated, Macbeth promises to 'drink a measure / The table round'. In many societies and religions, the sharing of a cup of wine, sometimes even called a 'loving-cup', symbolizes unity and fellowship; and so it is intended here. When Macbeth has stepped away from the table to speak to the murderer, Lady Macbeth calls him back, and reminds him of his duty as a host, adding that on such an occasion 'the sauce to meat is ceremony'. Macbeth brings chaos to Scotland, breaking up the harmony of a well-ordered country, just as he breaks up the state banquet 'With most admir'd disorder'.

Scene 5   It is a pity that this silly little scene has to be included in *Macbeth*. Shakespeare never wrote like this, and it was probably inserted into the play by some over-enthusiastic actor, who saw that the audiences enjoyed the witches' scenes, and decided to give them another. Or perhaps it is the work of an actor who found he had no part in the play, and so created the character of Hecate for himself, writing these lines, and five more in *Act 4*, Scene 1 (39-43). This person must also, I think, take the responsibility for the placing of Scene 6. This would be more appropriate coming *after* the visit to the witches, which should follow immediately after the banquet scene: Macbeth said then that he would call upon the witches 'tomorrow—And betimes I will', and he would not have postponed such an important errand.

Scene 6   Suspicion of Macbeth is growing. Lennox speaks here not as himself, an individual character, but with what we now call 'the voice of the people'. His words are innocent in meaning, but the exaggeration of tone directs the actor to make his speech heavily sarcastic—as, for example, in these lines:

> How it did grieve Macbeth! did he not straight
> In pious rage the two delinquents tear,
> That were the slaves of drink and thralls of sleep?

The unnamed Lord gives us information about Malcolm, and also makes the first reference in the play to the king of England, 'the most pious Edward', who is the complete opposite of Macbeth. The comparison will be developed in a later scene.

Act 4

Scene 1   We now see Macbeth receiving comfort from the three Apparitions that the witches call up. They appear in symbolic form. The first, 'an armed head', represents Macbeth's own head (wearing a helmet), as it is cut off and brought to Malcolm in *Act 5*, Scene 7. The 'bloody child' that comes next is Macduff, who had been 'untimely ripp'd' from his mother's womb (as he tells Macbeth in *Act 5*, Scene 7). And the last, the royal child with a tree in his hand, is Malcolm, the rightful king of Scotland, who approaches the palace at Dunsinane camouflaged with tree-branches (*Act 5*, Scene 4). Macbeth cannot interpret these symbols, but Shakespeare expects the audience to understand what is meant. This is 'dramatic irony'—when the truth of a situation is known to the audience but hidden from the characters in the play. There is dramatic irony, too, in the words spoken by the Apparitions, for again we understand the real meanings, while Macbeth can only understand the apparent meanings of the words. Macbeth, however, is in no doubt about the significance of the final 'show of Eight Kings'.

Scene 2   This pathetic scene in which Lady Macduff and her son are massacred shows us Macbeth's cruelty in action. When he plotted to kill Banquo's son, Fleance, he could justify the crime to himself by referring to the prophecy that Banquo's children should be kings. But he is in no danger from Lady Macduff or from her son; the crime is more dreadful because it is motiveless. Our knowledge of it helps us to find more dramatic irony in the scene that follows,

Scene 3   when Malcolm mistrusts Macduff chiefly because he cannot understand

> Why in that rawness left you wife and child—
> Those precious motives, those strong knots of love—
> Without leave-taking?

Macduff must prove his loyalty to Malcolm and to Scotland; then Malcolm must prove that he is worthy to be king. Again we are told of Edward the Confessor, and this time we hear of his divine gift of healing. This characteristic was not chosen by chance. Shakespeare uses many images of sickness; just a little later in this scene, he describes Scotland as a place where

>   good men's lives
> Expire before the flowers in their caps,
> Dying or ere they sicken.

In Act 5 Scene 2 Caithness recognizes Malcolm as the doctor who can cure Scotland's sickness, calling him 'the medicine of the sickly weal' (line 27).

We respond intellectually to this account of the English king, and to the concept of the monarch as some kind of physician, divinely appointed to safeguard the country's health. We respond emotionally to the next episode in this long scene as Ross breaks the bad news to Macduff. We feel the painful irony of Ross's evasive answer: 'they were well at peace when I did leave 'em'. If we had not seen Lady Macduff and her son, we should not be distressed; because of scene 2, we are able to share Macduff's own grief. I am always moved by Macduff's answer to Malcolm, who urges him to

> Dispute it like a man.

Macduff replies with dignity

> I shall do so;
> But I must also feel it like a man.

The word 'man' is being used in two senses. Malcolm intends it to mean 'bravely', but Macduff is thinking of a man as a human being, with tender emotions of love and grief, which must not be denied.

Act 5

Scene 1   The very next scene shows what happens when human emotions are denied. At the beginning of the play Lady Macbeth prayed that she should know 'no compunctious visitings of nature' (*1*, 5, 44) that might prevent her from murdering Duncan. Now she walks in her sleep, and her mind constantly re-lives the night of the murder. On that night she declared confidently that 'A little water clears us of this deed' (*2*, 2, 67), but now she knows that 'all the perfumes of Arabia will not sweeten this little hand'. It is the last time we see Lady Macbeth. Although the Doctor warns her lady-in-waiting to 'Remove from her the means of all annoyance', we learn later that 'by self and violent hands', she killed herself (*5*, 7, 99).

Scene 2   From now until the end of the play the action moves between the two armies—Malcolm's soldiers, steadily drawing closer to Dunsinane, and Macbeth's forces, besieged near the castle. Caithness and Angus discuss the strength of the enemy, and Angus offers a shrewd comment on Macbeth:

> Now does he feel his title
> Hang loose about him, like a giant's robe
> Upon a dwarfish thief.

This is not the first image of badly-fitting clothes. When Macbeth was given the title 'thane of Cawdor', soon after the witches had prophesied that it would be given to him, he stood apart from Banquo and the king's messengers; then Banquo laughed, and explained that Macbeth was like a man with new clothes:

> New honours come upon him,
> Like our strange garments, cleave not to their mould
> But with the aid of use.   (*1*, 3, 144-6)

Macbeth himself thought of the praises he had earned for his courage in terms of fine clothes,

> Which would be worn now in their newest gloss,
> Not cast aside so soon.   (*1*, 7, 34-5)

There are many such allusions throughout the play. They make us stop and think about the relationship between Macbeth and the honours he is 'wearing'. Has he won them, or stolen them? Will his 'clothes' fit, in time—or will they always be too big for him?

Scene 3   When he has heard the Doctor's medical opinion of his wife, Macbeth asks, with his grim humour, for a medical opinion on the state of the country. The Doctor is allowed the same humour when he closes the scene:

> Were I from Dunsinane away and clear,
> Profit again should hardly draw me here.

The situation is now so serious that only a sour joke (playing on the Elizabethan belief in the doctor's greed for gold) can ease the tension.

Scene 4 Birnam Wood begins to move; what seemed like witches' magic is seen to be elementary military tactics. Excitement and tension mount, as the soldiers come closer to Dunsinane. But Scene 5 Macbeth does not respond to the excitement: he has lost the capacity for feeling either fear or, as we see when he hears of his wife's death, grief. He speaks the most disillusioned words that Shakespeare ever wrote when he contemplates life's 'petty pace from day to day'. He still hopes that the witches' promises (made to him in *Act 4*, Scene 1) will protect him; but when he hears that 'The wood began to move' his confidence is shaken, and he begins

> To doubt the equivocation of the fiend
> That lies like truth.

At this point we should remember the 'equivocator' that the Porter joked about, long ago, in *Act 2*, Scene 3, and appreciate the way that this whole play insists on the difference between *being* and *seeming*, or between saying one thing and meaning another.

Scene 6 Continuous battle is now being waged, and the stage should never be empty. Macbeth is at last forced to confront Macduff, Scene 7 and also to confront the truth and admit that 'these juggling fiends' cannot be trusted. When the castle has been surrendered, Macbeth defeated, and victory proclaimed, Malcolm announces the beginning of a new reign. Order has now been restored to Scotland, and affairs will once again be conducted 'in measure, time, and place'.

Macbeth: The man

Who can tell us more about a man's character than his wife? Shakespeare allows Lady Macbeth to explain her husband's character as she understands it, and although she cannot see the *whole* truth, she tells us a great deal about Macbeth that *is* true. Two lines of her soliloquy in *Act 1*, Scene 5 are particularly significant:

> Thou wouldst be great,
> Art not without ambition, but without
> The illness should attend it.   (*1*, 5, 17-19)

By 'illness' Lady Macbeth means 'evil', but her metaphor is appropriate: Macbeth 'catches' evil, as one might catch a disease. The play shows how his symptoms develop, until there is no hope of a cure, and the man must die.

We hear a lot about Macbeth before he comes on to the stage, first from the Sergeant who has fought on his side, and then from Ross, who also speaks of Macbeth's courage in battle. These reports lead us to expect a noble warrior and a loyal subject to Duncan. We have only one slight doubt about Macbeth, and we are not able to explain quite what this is. We know that, somehow, he is associated with the witches; and this, surely, cannot be good.

Macbeth speaks very little when first the witches, and then Ross, hail him as 'thane of Cawdor'. Perhaps he is stunned to silence by his good fortune. But soon we hear him speak—or rather, think aloud, for he does not mean to be overheard:

> Glamis, and thane of Cawdor;
> The greatest is behind.   (*1*, 3, 116-17)

Very soon he begins to admit a 'suggestion', some 'horrible imaginings', and then he says to himself the word 'murder' (*1*, 3, 134; 138; 139). Once this word has been spoken, we must regard Macbeth with suspicion, and the suspicion grows when he confesses his 'black and deep desires' in the scene that follows

($1, 4, 51$). It is confirmed when his wife, speaking as though he were in the room with her, tells Macbeth that she knows he wants

> that which rather thou dost fear to do
> Than wishest should be undone.   ($1, 5, 23-4$)

It is not, however, cowardice that restrains Macbeth. At the end of *Act 1* he is wrestling with his conscience. He is acutely aware of the duty which he owes to Duncan:

> He's here in double trust:
> First, as I am his kinsman and his subject,
> Strong both against the deed; then as his host,
> Who should against his murderer shut the door,
> Not bear the knife myself.   ($1, 7, 12-16$)

These are profound reasons for curbing his ambition, but Macbeth continues the soliloquy. Even if he were not—as kinsman, subject, and host—in duty bound to defend Duncan, rather than harm him, there would still be enormous sin in killing the king. Macbeth appreciates Duncan's fine qualities—his humility and his integrity in carrying out to perfection the tasks of kingship; and he knows that to destroy such virtue would be a crime against heaven. He can appreciate Duncan's good qualities, and this is a virtue in Macbeth.

Before Lady Macbeth comes on to the scene, Macbeth has won a great victory over himself, and he is almost triumphant when he tells her, 'We will proceed no further in this business' ($1, 7, 31$).

But Lady Macbeth has no such conscience as her husband has. At this moment she is the stronger of the two, and Macbeth cannot stand up to her accusations that he is a coward, lacking in manliness, and a traitor to his word. He yields to her, and in order to prove himself a man in her eyes, submits to a woman's guidance.

After the murder of Duncan, Macbeth is horrified to think of what he has done. Again Shakespeare contrasts Macbeth and his wife in their attitudes to murder. Lady Macbeth is bold and confident, because she does not understand that the deed is morally wrong; her only concern is to destroy the evidence. Macbeth, however, awakens to a consciousness of guilt that will remain with him until his death.

Macbeth now has to act many parts. When the body of Duncan is discovered, he must appear as the loyal subject, appalled by the murder of his king. In speaking to the two Murderers whom he has hired to kill Banquo, he tries to show that he is a worthy ruler, distressed by injuries which have been inflicted on his subjects. And at the state banquet, probably his first public appearance since he was made king, he plays the part of host and friend to his thanes. He is not wholly successful in any of these roles. When the murder is discovered, he over-acts to such an extent that his wife tries to draw attention from him by fainting. The Murderers are not interested in his efforts to justify the murder of Banquo: they have been hired to kill a man, and they will do the job they are paid to do. And the banquet is ruined for Macbeth by the appearance of Banquo's Ghost.

Macbeth appears again as himself (that is, not playing any 'part') at the end of *Act 3*, Scene 4, when he and his wife face each other across the remains of their banquet. He now knows that 'blood will have blood' (*1*, 4, 122), and that the first murder is *only* the first. A new character is emerging—a man who is so desperate that he must act and not stop to consider the reasons for acting:

Strange things I have in head that will to hand,
Which must be acted ere they may be scann'd.

(*3*, 4, 139–40)

The last line here refers to an actor's part in a play, which ought to be 'scann'd'—that is, learned—before it is performed. With this comparison, Macbeth is beginning to recognize an unreality about his life.

The new Macbeth confronts the witches and demands to be answered; the answers give him a feeling of confidence which we, the audience, know to be unfounded. But Macbeth trusts no-one. He has no faith in the loyalty of the thanes, and sets spies on each one of them (see *3*, 4, 131–2); now it seems that he will not trust even the witches and their 'masters', for he is determined to 'make assurance double sure' (*4*, 1, 83) by slaughtering Macduff's entire family.

We do not see Macbeth for some time after his appearance in this scene with the witches. We hear a lot about him—and everything that we hear tells us that Macbeth has become a cruel tyrant, and that he has changed Scotland into a country 'Almost afraid to know itself' (*4*, 3, 165). There are more rumours to be heard when Malcolm's army moves towards Dunsinane; opinions about Macbeth vary:

Some say he's mad; others, that lesser hate him,
Do call it valiant fury.   (*5*, 2, 13–14)

He is indeed madly self-confident, believing that he is invincible:

> Till Birnam wood remove to Dunsinane
> I cannot taint with fear. What's the boy Malcolm?
> Was he not born of woman?   (5, 3, 2–4)

Alone, however, Macbeth is neither mad nor furious. He feels old and lonely:

>   my way of life
> Is fall'n into the sere, the yellow leaf;
> And that which should accompany old age,
> As honour, love, obedience, troops of friends,
> I must not look to have.   (5, 3, 22–6)

Seyton tells him that his wife is dead, but he cannot grieve for her. Life has no meaning for him, and once again he sees himself as an actor,

> That struts and frets his hour upon the stage,
> And then is heard no more.   (5, 5, 25–6)

He has lost everything, and when he hears of the 'moving grove' (5, 5, 38) he knows that he is defeated.

Macbeth chooses to die in battle, 'with harness on our back' (5, 5, 52), and the decision perhaps revives a spark of our former respect for the mighty warrior. At last he is challenged by Macduff, and he is reluctant to fight:

> Of all men else I have avoided thee:
> But get thee back, my soul is too much charg'd
> With blood of thine already.   (5, 7, 33–5)

How should we interpret this? The first of the Apparitions told Macbeth to 'Beware Macduff'—is this why he has avoided him? Or is it guilt that has kept Macbeth from coming face-to-face with the man whose wife and children have been so brutally murdered? Is conscience returning with courage?

Shakespeare's Verse

Shakespeare's plays are mainly written in 'blank verse', the form preferred by most dramatists in the sixteenth and early seventeenth centuries. It is a very flexible medium, which is capable — like the human speaking voice — of a wide range of tones. Basically the lines, which are unrhymed, are ten syllables long. The syllables have alternating stresses, just like normal English speech; and they divide into five 'feet'. The technical name for this is 'iambic pentameter'.

> **Macbeth**
> So foúl and faír a dáy I haʋe not seén.
> **Banquo**
> How fár is't cáll'd to Fórres? Wħat are thése,
> So wiħer'd añd so wíld in théir attíre,
> That loók not liķe th'inhábitants ó' the eaŕth,
> And yét are oñ't? Live yóu? Or aŕe you aught
> That mán may quéstion? Yóu seem tó understánd
>   me,
> By eaćh at onće her chóppy fiñger láying
> Upón her skínny liṗs: you shóuld be woṁen,
> And yét your beárds forbíd me tó inteŕpret
> That yóu are só.
> **Macbeth**
> Speak, íf you cań; what aŕe you?

1, 3, 38–47

Here the pentameter accommodates a variety of speech tones — Macbeth is casual in his conversation about the weather; Banquo is surprised at the appearance of these creatures, and fearful that they may be supernatural beings; he is comforted when they seem to understand him; and he can even make a nervous joke about their beards. Macbeth, speaking with some authority, completes a line started by Banquo — and so identifies himself with the other's feelings. Some words in Banquo's speech have had to be elided ('th'inhabitants', 'o' the'), but this is usual in English — especially when the speaker is under pressure from some emotion (and Banquo is *very* surprised!).

In this quotation, the lines are regular in length and normal in iambic stress pattern. Sometimes Shakespeare deviates from the norm, writing lines that are longer or shorter than ten syllables, and varying the stress patterns for unusual emphasis. The verse line sometimes contains the grammatical unit of meaning — 'So wither'd and so wild in their attire' — thus allowing for a pause at the end of the line, before a new idea is started; at other times, the sense runs on from one line to the next — 'are you aught That man may question'. This makes for the natural fluidity of speech, avoiding monotony but still maintaining the iambic rhythm.

Date and Text

Macbeth was probably written in the summer of 1606. The evidence for this comes partly from within the play itself. In *Act 2*, Scene 3, the drunken Porter visualizes himself as the 'porter of hell-gate' who admits 'an equivocator, that could swear in both the scales against either scale; who committed treason enough for God's sake, yet could not equivocate to heaven' (lines 9–11). The reference is to Father Garnet, a Jesuit priest who was tried and executed in the spring of 1606 for his part in the Gunpowder Plot which had threatened to blow up the King and the Houses of Parliament on 5th November in the previous year.

The play did not appear in print before the First Folio collection of Shakespeare's *Works*, which was published in 1623.

Characters in the play

Duncan	*King of Scotland*
Malcolm **Donalbain**	*his sons*
Macbeth **Banquo**	*commanders of the Scottish army*
Macduff **Lennox** **Ross** **Menteith** **Angus** **Caithness**	*thanes of Scotland* (*thane :* a Scottish nobleman, just below the rank of earl in the English nobility.)
Fleance	*Banquo's son*
Boy	*Macduff's son*
Seyton	*an officer attending Macbeth*
Siward	*Earl of Northumberland, commander of the English army*
Young Siward	*his son*
Lady Macbeth	
Lady Macduff	

A Sergeant
A Porter
An Old Man
Three Murderers
An English Doctor
A Scottish Doctor
A Gentlewoman attending Lady Macbeth
Three Witches
Hecate   *goddess and queen of witches*
The Ghost of Banquo
Apparitions
Lords, Attendants, Soldiers, Attendants, Messengers

Act 1

Act 1   scene 1
A Prologue of evil. The witches plan
to meet Macbeth when the fighting has
finished.

 moor : a wasteland area.

3 *hurlyburly :* fighting.

8 *Graymalkin :* grey cat.

9 *Paddock :* toad.

10 *Anon :* at once—I'm coming.

Scene 1 *On the moor*

> *Thunder and lightning. Enter three* Witches

First Witch
When shall we three meet again
In thunder, lightning, or in rain?
Second Witch
When the hurlyburly's done,
When the battle's lost and won.
Third Witch
5 That will be ere the set of sun.
First Witch
Where the place?
Second Witch   Upon the heath.
Third Witch
There to meet with Macbeth.
First Witch
I come, Graymalkin!
Second Witch
Paddock calls.
10 **Third Witch**   Anon.
All
Fair is foul, and foul is fair:
Hover through the fog and filthy air.   [*Exeunt*

[handwritten: To award someone a little after they kill them - woman]

Act I scene 2

The good King Duncan hears news of the battle. He is told how bravely Macbeth and Banquo have fought first against Macdonwald and his band of rebels; and then against the Norwegians and the Scottish traitor, the Thane of Cawdor. He declares that Macbeth shall be rewarded with the title of 'Thane of Cawdor'.

Alarum : a battle call on a trumpet; this shows that the scene is now a military camp

2 *As . . . plight :* his wounded condition suggests.

3 *newest state :* latest condition.

5 *'Gainst my captivity :* so that the enemy did not capture me.

6 *broil :* conflict

8 *spent :* exhausted.

9 *choke their art :* hinder each other's skill.

9-14 The rebel Scot, Macdonwald—who is fit only to be a traitor because he has so many vices—had the assistance ('is supplied') of footsoldiers ('kerns') and cavalry ('gallowglasses') from Ireland and the Hebrides. Fortune, like a prostitute, seemed to be also on his side.

17 *steel :* sword.

18 *smok'd :* steamed. *[handwritten: bad/luck is a whore]*

19 *minion :* favourite.

21-2 Macbeth did not part from Macdonwald until he had ripped him open from the navel to the jaws.

25-8 But just as storms arise from the east (where the sun rises), so from the place where we expected hope, further trouble arose.

[handwritten: mc donnal wald is a rebel]

Scene 2. *A camp near Forres*

Alarum. Enter King Duncan, Malcolm, Donalbain, Lennox, *with* Attendants, *meeting a bleeding* Sergeant

Duncan

    What bloody man is that? He can report,
As seemeth by his plight, of the revolt
The newest state.

Malcolm   This is the sergeant
Who, like a good and hardy soldier, fought
5 'Gainst my captivity. Hail, brave friend!
Say to the king the knowledge of the broil
As thou didst leave it.

Sergeant   Doubtful it stood;
As two spent swimmers, that do cling together
And choke their art. The merciless Macdonwald—
10 Worthy to be a rebel, for to that
The multiplying villainies of nature
Do swarm upon him—from the western isles
Of kerns and gallowglasses is supplied;
And fortune, on his damned quarrel smiling,
15 Show'd like a rebel's whore: but all's too weak;
For brave Macbeth—well he deserves that
    name—
Disdaining fortune, with his brandish'd steel
Which smok'd with bloody execution,
Like valour's minion carv'd out his passage
20 Till he fac'd the slave;
Which ne'er shook hands, nor bade farewell to him,
Till he unseam'd him from the nave to the chaps,
And fix'd his head upon our battlements.

Duncan

O valiant cousin! worthy gentleman!

Sergeant

25 As whence the sun 'gins his reflection
Shipwracking storms and direful thunders break,
So from that spring, whence comfort seem'd to
    come,
Discomfort swells. Mark, King of Scotland, mark:
No sooner justice had, with valour arm'd,

30 Made these villains run away.	30 Compell'd these skipping kerns to trust their heels, But the Norweyan lord, surveying vantage,
31-3 Sveno the Norwegian seized his chance, and with fresh arms and more men made a new attack.	With furbish'd arms and new supplies of men Began a fresh assault.

        Duncan   Dismay'd not this
Our captains, Macbeth and Banquo?
        Sergeant ·Sarcasm   Yes;

35 As sparrows eagles, or the hare the lion.

36 *sooth* : truth.	If I say sooth, I must report they were
37 *double cracks* : a double load of ammunition.	As cannons overcharg'd with double cracks; So they Doubly redoubled strokes upon the foe: -pity

40-2 The sergeant cannot tell whether Macbeth and Banquo thought they would swim in blood, or make this scene of bloodshed as memorable ('memorize') as Golgotha (where Christ was crucified).	40 Except they meant to bathe in reeking wounds, Or memorize another Golgotha, I cannot tell— But I am faint, my gashes cry for help. **Duncan** So well thy words become thee as thy wounds;
44-5 The soldier's words are as suitable for him as his wounds: both taste ('smack') of honour.	45 They smack of honour both. Go, get him surgeons.

                      [*Exit* Sergeant, *with other soldiers*

           Enter Ross
Who comes here?
        Malcolm   The worthy Thane of Ross.
        Lennox
What a haste looks through his eyes! So should he
   look
That seems to speak things strange.
        Ross   God save the king!
        Duncan
Whence cam'st thou, worthy thane?
        Ross   From Fife, great king;

47 His eyes show he is in a hurry.	

50 *flout* : scorn (the Norwegian flags have no right to be at Fife).	50 Where the Norweyan banners flout the sky And fan our people cold. Norway himself,
51-9 The king of Norway, with a fearful army and supported by the Thane of Cawdor, began to fight. Then Macbeth, who appeared like the husband of Bellona, goddess of war, clothed in strong armour ('lapp'd in proof'), opposed him with sword and courage like his own, until we won the battle.	With terrible numbers, Assisted by that most disloyal traitor, The Thane of Cawdor, began a dismal conflict; 55 Till that Bellona's bridegroom, lapp'd in proof, Confronted him with self-comparisons,

Point against point, rebellious arm 'gainst arm,
Curbing his lavish spirit: and, to conclude,
The victory fell on us.

Duncan   Great happiness!

Ross
60 That now
Sweno, the Norways' king, craves composition;
Nor would we deign him burial of his men
Till he disbursed, at Saint Colme's Inch,
Ten thousand dollars to our general use.

Duncan
65 No more that Thane of Cawdor shall deceive
Our bosom interest. Go pronounce his present
death,
And with his former title greet Macbeth.

His title →

Ross
I'll see it done.

Duncan
What he hath lost noble Macbeth hath won.

[*Exeunt*

61 *craves composition :* begs for peace.

63 *disbursed :* paid.

66 *bosom interest :* love.
present : immediate.

Act 1   scene 3
The witches assemble, and prepare to
meet Macbeth, who is travelling with
Banquo towards the king's camp at
Forres. The two men hear the witches'
prophecies with amazement, and then
Ross comes to them with a message
from Duncan.

6 *Aroint thee :* Go away!
rump-fed ronyon : fat-bottomed old
woman.

Scene 3 *On the moor*

Thunder. Enter the three Witches
First Witch
Where hast thou been, sister?
Second Witch
Killing swine.
Third Witch
Sister, where thou?
First Witch
A sailor's wife had chestnuts in her lap,
5 And munch'd, and munch'd, and munch'd: 'Give
me,' quoth I.
'Aroint thee, witch!' the rump-fed ronyon cries.
Her husband's to Aleppo gone, master o' the Tiger:
But in a sieve I'll thither sail,
And, like a rat without a tail,
10 I'll do, I'll do, and I'll do.
Second Witch
I'll give thee a wind,

First Witch
Th'art kind.
Third Witch
And I another.
First Witch
I myself have all the other;
15 And the very ports they blow,
All the quarters that they know
I' the shipman's card.
I'll drain him dry as hay:
Sleep shall neither night nor day
20 Hang upon his pent-house lid;
He shall live a man forbid.
Weary sev'n-nights nine times nine
Shall he dwindle, peak and pine:
Though his bark cannot be lost,
25 Yet it shall be tempest-tost.
Look what I have.
Second Witch
Show me, show me.
First Witch
Here I have a pilot's thumb,
Wreck'd as homeward he did come.

[*A drum beats*

Third Witch
30 A drum! a drum!
Macbeth doth come.
All
The weird sisters, hand in hand,
Posters of the sea and land,
Thus do go about, about:
35 Thrice to thine, and thrice to mine,
And thrice again, to make up nine.
Peace! the charm's wound up.

Enter Macbeth *and* Banquo

Macbeth
So foul and fair a day I have not seen.
Banquo
How far is 't call'd to Forres? What are these,
40 So wither'd and so wild in their attire,
That look not like th' inhabitants o' the earth,
And yet are on 't? Live you? or are you aught
That man may question? You seem to under-
stand me,

14   *the other :* the other winds.

17   *shipman's card :* compass.

20   *pent-house lid :* eyelid (which slopes like a shed leaning on the side of a house).
21   *forbid :* accursed.

24   *bark :* ship.

32   *weird :* supernatural.
33   *Posters :* fast travellers.

44   *choppy* : chapped (rough and red).

By each at once her choppy finger laying
45 Upon her skinny lips : you should be women,
And yet your beards forbid me to interpret
That you are so.
> **Macbeth**   Speak, if you can : what are you?
> **First Witch**
All hail, Macbeth! hail to thee, Thane of Glamis!
> **Second Witch**
All hail, Macbeth! hail to thee, Thane of Cawdor!
> **Third Witch**
50 All hail, Macbeth! that shalt be King hereafter.
> **Banquo**
Good sir, why do you start, and seem to fear
Things that do sound so fair? I' the name of truth,

53-4   Are you imaginary, or as real as you
seem to be?

54-7   You greet my friend with his
present title, with prophecy of future
nobility, and with promise of royalty,
so that he seems amazed with it all.

Are ye fantastical, or that indeed
Which outwardly ye show? My noble partner
55 You greet with present grace, and great prediction
Of noble having and of royal hope,
That he seems rapt withal : to me you speak not.
If you can look into the seeds of time,
And say which grain will grow and which will not,
60 Speak then to me, who neither beg nor fear,
Your favours nor your hate.
> **First Witch**
Hail!
> **Second Witch**
Hail!
> **Third Witch**
Hail!
> **First Witch**
65 Lesser than Macbeth, and greater.
> **Second Witch**
Not so happy, yet much happier.
> **Third Witch**
Thou shalt get kings, though thou be none :

67   *get* : beget, be father of.

So, all hail, Macbeth and Banquo!
> **First Witch**
Banquo and Macbeth, all hail!

Telling Banquo that he will not be a king but his kids will

70   *imperfect :* unintelligible.

72   *the Thane of Cawdor lives.* Macbeth does not know of the Thane's treachery. Angus explains (lines 109-16) that he had conspired in secret with the king of Norway.

74   *Stands . . . belief :* is unbelievable.

81   *corporal :* solid, having a body.
82   *Would . . . stay'd!* I wish that they had stayed.

84   *the insane root :* hemlock, a drug that makes men mad.

91   *venture :* daring.
92-3   The king does not know whether to praise Macbeth or say how amazed he is.

96   *afeard :* afraid.

98   *post :* messenger.
98-9   The messengers all reported praise for what Macbeth had done in the defence of his country.

Macbeth

70 Stay, you imperfect speakers, tell me more :
    By Sinel's death I know I am Thane of Glamis ;
    But how of Cawdor? the Thane of Cawdor lives,
    A prosperous gentleman ; and to be king
    Stands not within the prospect of belief,
75 No more than to be Cawdor. Say from whence
    You owe this strange intelligence? or why
    Upon this blasted heath you stop our way
    With such prophetic greeting? Speak, I charge you.
    [Witches *vanish*

Banquo
    The earth hath bubbles, as the water has,
80 And these are of them. Whither are they vanish'd?

Macbeth
    Into the air, and what seem'd corporal melted,
    As breath into the wind. Would they had stay'd!

Banquo
    Were such things here as we do speak about?
    Or have we eaten on the insane root
85 That takes the reason prisoner?

Macbeth
    Your children shall be kings.
Banquo   You shall be king.
Macbeth
    And Thane of Cawdor too ; went it not so?
Banquo
    To the self-same tune and words. Who's here?

    Enter Ross *and* Angus

Ross
    The king hath happily receiv'd, Macbeth,
90 The news of thy success ; and when he reads
    Thy personal venture in the rebels' fight,
    His wonders and his praises do contend
    Which should be thine or his. Silenc'd with that,
    In viewing o'er the rest o' the self-same day,
95 He finds thee in the stout Norweyan ranks,
    Nothing afeard of what thyself didst make,
    Strange images of death. As thick as hail
    Came post with post, and every one did bear

101   Ross and Angus bring thanks
       from Duncan to greet Macbeth
       as he comes before the king, but
       these thanks are not the only
       payment he will receive.
104   *earnest* : a token, promising more
       reward.
106   *addition* : additional title.

111   *combin'd* : allied.

112   *line* : strengthen (as the lining
       strengthens a garment).
113   *vantage* : advantage (perhaps the
       traitor gave the foreign enemies a base
       in Scotland from which they could
       attack).
115   *treasons capital* : treasons which
       are punishable by death.
117   *the greatest is behind* : the greatest
       of the three prophecies is the last of
       them, and has not happened yet.
       pains : trouble.

120   *trusted home* : trusted completely.
121   *enkindle* : set your hopes on fire.

123-6 Often, to bring about our
       damnation, the agents of evil tell us
       simple truths, so that we trust them;
       then they deceive us in important
       matters.
127   *Cousins* : Friends.

Thy praises in his kingdom's great defence,
100 And pour'd them down before him.
                Angus   We are sent
     To give thee from our royal master thanks;
     Only to herald thee into his sight,
     Not pay thee.
                Ross
     And, for an earnest of a greater honour,
105 He bade me, from him, call thee Thane of Cawdor:
     In which addition, hail, most worthy Thane!
     For it is thine.
                Banquo [*Aside*] What! can the devil speak true
                Macbeth
     The Thane of Cawdor lives: why do you dress me
     In borrow'd robes?
                Angus   Who was the Thane lives yet;
110 But under heavy judgment bears that life
     Which he deserves to lose. Whether he was
       combin'd
     With those of Norway, or did line the rebel
     With hidden help or vantage, or that with both
     He labour'd in his country's wreck, I know not;
115 But treasons capital, confess'd and prov'd,
     Have overthrown him.
                Macbeth
              [*Aside*] Glamis, and Thane of Cawdor:
     The greatest is behind. [*To* Ross *and* Angus]
                              Thanks for your pains.
     [*To* Banquo] Do you not hope your children shall
       be kings,
     When those that gave the Thane of Cawdor to me
120 Promis'd no less to them?
                Banquo   That, trusted home,
     Might yet enkindle you unto the crown,
     Besides the Thane of Cawdor. But 'tis strange:
     And oftentimes, to win us to our harm,
     The instruments of darkness tell us truths,
125 Win us with honest trifles, to betray's
     In deepest consequence.
     Cousins, a word, I pray you.

128-9   Macbeth sees his future before him as though it were a mighty play on the theme of kingship.

130   *soliciting* : persuasion.

136   *seated* : firmly fixed.

139-42   Macbeth's mind, which thinks of murder as merely fantastical, disturbs his whole being. He can do nothing because he is wondering what will happen ('surmise'). Only the future ('what is not') is real to him.

142   *rapt* : amazed, lost in his own thoughts.

144   *Without my stir* : Without any effort from me.

145-6   New clothes do not fit ('cleave to') our bodies until we are accustomed to them.

146-7   Let what is going to happen, happen; even the hardest day comes to an end.

148   *stay* : wait.

150-2   His memory is like a book, which he reads every day, and he will always remember their efforts ('pains').

154   *interim* : meanwhile. Between the present, and a future meeting with Banquo, Macbeth will have had time to think about what has happened ('chanc'd').

155   *free* : honest.

Macbeth [*Aside*]   Two truths are told,
As happy prologues to the swelling act
Of the imperial theme. [*Aloud*] I thank you, gentlemen.
130 [*Aside*] This supernatural soliciting
Cannot be ill, cannot be good; if ill,
Why hath it given me earnest of success,
Commencing in a truth? I am Thane of Cawdor:
If good, why do I yield to that suggestion
135 Whose horrid image doth unfix my hair
And make my seated heart knock at my ribs,
Against the use of nature? Present fears
Are less than horrible imaginings;
My thought, whose murder yet is but fantastical,
140 Shakes so my single state of man that function
Is smother'd in surmise, and nothing is
But what is not.
Banquo   Look, how our partner's rapt.
Macbeth
[*Aside*] If chance will have me king, why, chance
may crown me,
Without my stir.
Banquo   New honours come upon him,
145 Like our strange garments, cleave not to their mould
But with the aid of use.
Macbeth [*Aside*]   Come what come may,
Time and the hour runs through the roughest day.
Banquo
Worthy Macbeth, we stay upon your leisure.
Macbeth
Give me your favour: my dull brain was wrought
150 With things forgotten. Kind gentlemen, your pains
Are register'd where every day I turn
The leaf to read them. Let us toward the King.
[*To* Banquo] Think upon what hath chanc'd; and,
at more time,
The interim having weigh'd it, let us speak
155 Our free hearts each to other.
Banquo   Very gladly.

Macbeth

Till then, enough. Come, friends.   *[Exeunt*

Act 1   scene 4

Duncan receives Macbeth and Banquo, and tells the company that his son Malcolm is next heir to the throne of Scotland.

Flourish : Fanfare, heralding the royal procession.

2   *in commission :* in charge of the execution.

     liege : lord.

6   *set forth :* showed.

9   *studied in :* practised.
10   *ow'd :* owned.
11-12 One cannot learn to know a man's mind by looking at his face.

16-20 Macbeth, in his deserving, is far ahead of any payment. Duncan wishes he had deserved less, so that his thanks and reward might be more in proportion.

21   *thy due :* due to you.

23   *pays itself :* is its own reward.

26-7 It is no more than our duty to do everything we can to ensure the safety of your love and honour.

Scene 4 *Forres. A room in the palace*

> *Flourish. Enter* Duncan, Malcolm,
> Donalbain, Lennox, *and* Attendants

Duncan

Is execution done on Cawdor? Are not
Those in commission yet return'd?

Malcolm   My liege,

They are not yet come back; but I have spoke
With one that saw him die; who did report
5 That very frankly he confess'd his treasons,
Implor'd your highness' pardon, and set forth
A deep repentance. Nothing in his life
Became him like the leaving it; he died
As one that had been studied in his death,
10 To throw away the dearest thing he ow'd,
As 'twere a careless trifle.

Duncan   There's no art

To find the mind's construction in the face:
He was a gentleman on whom I built
An absolute trust.

> *Enter* Macbeth, Banquo, Ross, *and* Angus
> O worthiest cousin!

15 The sin of my ingratitude even now
Was heavy on me. Thou art so far before,
That swiftest wing of recompense is slow
To overtake thee; would thou hadst less deserv'd,
That the proportion both of thanks and payment
20 Might have been mine! Only I have left to say,
More is thy due than more than all can pay.

Macbeth

The service and the loyalty I owe,
In doing it, pays itself. Your highness' part
Is to receive our duties; and our duties
25 Are to your throne and state, children and servants;
Which do but what they should, by doing every-
    thing
Safe toward your love and honour.

Duncan   Welcome hither:
I have begun to plant thee, and will labour
To make thee full of growing. Noble Banquo,
30 That hast no less deserv'd, nor must be known
No less to have done so, let me infold thee
And hold thee to my heart.
        Banquo   There if I grow,
The harvest is your own.
        Duncan   My plenteous joys
Wanton in fulness, seek to hide themselves
35 In drops of sorrow. Sons, kinsmen, thanes,
And you whose places are the nearest, know
We will establish our estate upon
Our eldest, Malcolm, whom we name hereafter
The Prince of Cumberland; which honour must
40 Not unaccompanied invest him only,
But signs of nobleness, like stars, shall shine
On all deservers. [*To* Macbeth] From hence to
        Inverness,
And bind us further to you.
        Macbeth
The rest is labour, which is not us'd for you:
45 I'll be myself the harbinger, and make joyful
The hearing of my wife with your approach;
So, humbly take my leave.
        Duncan   My worthy Cawdor!
        Macbeth
[*Aside*] The Prince of Cumberland! that is a step
On which I must fall down, or else o'er-leap,
50 For in my way it lies. Stars, hide your fires!
Let not light see my black and deep desires;
The eye wink at the hand; yet let that be
Which the eye fears, when it is done, to see. [*Exit*
        Duncan
True, worthy Banquo; he is full so valiant,
55 And in his commendations I am fed;
It is a banquet to me. Let's after him,
Whose care is gone before to bid us welcome:
It is a peerless kinsman.   [*Flourish. Exeunt*

34   *Wanton :* Unrestrained.

36   *the nearest :* nearest to the throne, in line of succession.
37-42 Duncan names Malcolm as his successor, giving him the title 'Prince of Cumberland' (just as the Prince of Wales is heir to the English throne). Malcolm will not be the only one to be honoured; titles will be bestowed on all who deserve them.
42   *Inverness :* i.e. Macbeth's castle.
43   *bind us further :* increase our debt.

44   Resting-time is more like hard work, when it is not used for the king.
45   *harbinger :* herald.

52   *The eye wink at the hand :* let the eye not see what the hand is doing.

58   *peerless :* without an equal.

Act 1   scene 5
Lady Macbeth reads her husband's
letter; then she and Macbeth talk of
their plans.

5   *rapt :* amazed.

8   *coming on of time :* future.

10   *deliver thee :* report to you.

11   *dues of rejoicing :* your share of the
     rejoicing.

Scene 5 *Inverness. A room in Macbeth's castle*

Enter Lady Macbeth, *reading a letter*
Lady Macbeth
*'They met me in the day of success ; and I have learned
by the perfectest report, they have more in them than
mortal knowledge. When I burned in desire to question
them further, they made themselves air, into which they*
5 *vanished. Whiles I stood rapt in the wonder of it, came
missives from the king, who all-hailed me, "Thane of
Cawdor" ; by which title, before, these weird sisters
saluted me, and referred me to the coming on of time,
with, "Hail, king that shalt be !" This have I thought*
10 *good to deliver thee, my dearest partner of greatness,
that thou mightest not lose the dues of rejoicing, by
being ignorant of what greatness is promised thee. Lay
it to thy heart, and farewell.'*

Glamis thou art, and Cawdor; and shalt be

15 What thou art promis'd. Yet do I fear thy nature;
It is too full o' the milk of human kindness
To catch the nearest way. Thou wouldst be great,
Art not without ambition, but without
The illness should attend it; what thou wouldst
   highly,

20 That wouldst thou holily; wouldst not play false,
And yet wouldst wrongly win; thou'dst have, great
   Glamis,
That which cries, 'Thus thou must do', if thou
   have it;
And that which rather thou dost fear to do
Than wishest should be undone. Hie thee hither,

25 That I may pour my spirits in thine ear,
And chastise with the valour of my tongue
All that impedes thee from the golden round,
Which fate and metaphysical aid doth seem
To have thee crown'd withal.

Enter a Messenger
                           What is your tidings?
Messenger

30 The king comes here to-night.
Lady Macbeth   Thou 'rt mad to say it.
Is not thy master with him? who, were't so,
Would have inform'd for preparation.
Messenger
So please you, it is true: our thane is coming;
One of my fellows had the speed of him,

35 Who, almost dead for breath, had scarcely more
Than would make up his message.
Lady Macbeth   Give him tending;
He brings great news. [*Exit* Messenger] The
   raven himself is hoarse
That croaks the fatal entrance of Duncan
Under my battlements. Come, you spirits

40 That tend on mortal thoughts! unsex me here,
And fill me from the crown to the toe top-full
Of direst cruelty; make thick my blood,
Stop up the access and passage to remorse,
That no compunctious visitings of nature

19   *illness . . . it :* evil that must accompany
ambition.

22   *That :* i.e. the crown.

26   *chastise :* drive away.
27   *golden round :* crown.
28   *metaphysical :* supernatural (i.e. helped
by the witches).

29   *tidings :* news.

31-2   Macbeth would have told her that
the king was coming, so that she could
make preparations.

34   *had the speed of him :* travelled
faster than he did.

36   *tending :* care, attention.

40   *tend :* attend, wait.
unsex me : take away all that makes
me a woman (such as tenderness, love,
and pity).

42   *direst :* worst.

42-6   *make . . . and it :* make me insensitive,
by blocking up all the pathways by
which remorse can reach my heart, so
that no natural feelings of conscience
make me hesitate in my wicked ('fell')
plans, or come between my scheme and
the carrying-out ('th' effect') of this
scheme.

45 Shake my fell purpose, nor keep peace between
Th' effect and it! Come to my woman's breasts,
And take my milk for gall, you murdering ministers,
Wherever in your sightless substances
You wait on nature's mischief! Come, thick night,
50 And pall thee in the dunnest smoke of hell,
That my keen knife see not the wound it makes,
Nor heaven peep through the blanket of the dark,
To cry, 'Hold, hold!'

Enter Macbeth
            Great Glamis! worthy Cawdor!
Greater than both, by the all-hail hereafter!
55 Thy letters have transported me beyond
This ignorant present, and I feel now
The future in the instant.
    Macbeth   My dearest love,
Duncan comes here to-night.
    Lady Macbeth   And when goes hence?
    Macbeth
To-morrow, as he purposes.
    Lady Macbeth   O never
60 Shall sun that morrow see!
Your face, my thane, is as a book where men
May read strange matters. To beguile the time,
Look like the time; bear welcome in your eye,
Your hand, your tongue: look like the innocent
    flower
65 But be the serpent under 't. He that's coming
Must be provided for; and you shall put
This night's great business into my dispatch;
Which shall to all our nights and days to come
Give solely sovereign sway and masterdom.
    Macbeth
70 We will speak further.
    Lady Macbeth   Only look up clear;
To alter favour ever is to fear.
Leave all the rest to me.   *[Exeunt*

47 *gall*: a bitter liquid, secreted in the liver.
48 *sightless*: invisible. Although the 'spirits' that Lady Macbeth invokes are real—they have 'substances'—they cannot be seen.
50 *pall*: shroud.
    dunnest: darkest.

54 *all-hail hereafter*: future prophecy.

57 *The future in the instant*. She is transported, in her imagination, into the future, and feels that this is already present ('in the instant').

62 *beguile*: deceive.
63 *Look like the time*: put on the appropriate appearance (which now is that of the welcoming host).

67 *dispatch*: management.

69 *solely sovereign sway*: nothing less than the power of a king.

70 *clear*: with an honest face.
71 Fear always shows itself in a change of expression.

Act 1 scene 6

Duncan and his court arrive at Macbeth's castle, and are welcomed by Lady Macbeth.

1   *seat* : situation.

2   *Nimbly* : freshly.

4   *martlet* : house-martin, a bird that often nests in churches.

      approve : prove.

5   *mansionry* : building.

6-8 The birds' nests hang (are 'pendent') on every convenient ('of vantage') jutting-out piece of the architecture of the castle, and these nests are the cradles for the young birds.

11-14 'I am sometimes embarrassed by the love that is shown to me ("follows us"), but I am always ("still") grateful, because it *is* love. In this I am teaching you to ask God to reward ("'eyld" = yield) me for the trouble ("pains") that *you* are having to take, and also to thank *me* for that trouble.' In this polite joke with Lady Macbeth, Duncan suggests that she will be a better person for this trouble, and therefore she should thank him for giving her the chance to improve.

15   If every part were done twice, and then twice again.

18   *those of old* : those honours bestowed in the past.

19   *late* : recent.

20   *hermits*. Lady Macbeth and her husband will be like holy men who offer prayers for their benefactors.

21   *cours'd* : chased.

      at the heels : closely.

Scene 6 *Outside Macbeth's castle*

> *Music and torches. Enter* Duncan,
> Malcolm, Donalbain, Banquo, Lennox,
> Macduff, Ross, Angus, *and* Attendants

Duncan

This castle hath a pleasant seat; the air
Nimbly and sweetly recommends itself
Unto our gentle senses.

  Banquo   This guest of summer,
The temple-haunting martlet, does approve,
5 By his lov'd mansionry, that the heaven's breath
Smells wooingly here: no jutty, frieze,
Buttress, nor coign of vantage, but this bird
Hath made his pendent bed and procreant cradle:
Where they most breed and haunt, I have observ'd
10 The air is delicate.

> *Enter* Lady Macbeth

  Duncan   See, see, our honour'd hostess!
The love that follows us sometime is our trouble,
Which still we thank as love. Herein I teach you
How you shall bid God 'eyld us for your pains,
And thank us for your trouble.

  Lady Macbeth   All our service,
15 In every point twice done, and then done double,
Were poor and single business, to contend
Against those honours deep and broad, wherewith
Your majesty loads our house: for those of old,
And the late dignities heap'd up to them,
20 We rest your hermits.

  Duncan   Where's the Thane of Cawdor?
We cours'd him at the heels, and had a purpose
To be his purveyor; but he rides well,
And his great love, sharp as his spur, hath holp him
To his home before us. Fair and noble hostess,
25 We are your guest to-night.

  Lady Macbeth   Your servants ever
Have theirs, themselves, and what is theirs, in compt,
To make their audit at your highness' pleasure,
Still to return your own.

22   *purveyor :* the official who went
       before a king to arrange for his
       reception.
23   *holp :* helped.
25-8   The king's servants hold everything
       in trust ('in compt') for the king, and
       they will give an account ('make . . .
       audit') whenever the king asks for one,
       and always ('still') return everything
       back to him.
31   *By your leave.* A courteous remark:
       Duncan may perhaps kiss Lady
       Macbeth's hand, or take her arm, and
       go into the castle with her.

Act 1   scene 7

Macbeth prepares for murder. He
knows that this is a great sin, but his wife
forces him to do the deed.

1-2   *If . . . quickly :* if the business of the
       murder were ended ('done') as soon as
       the murder is performed ('done'), then
       it would be a good thing to have it
       carried out ('done') quickly.
2-4   *if . . . success :* if the assassination
       could prevent ('trammel' = entangle,
       enmesh) any further consequences, and
       succeed as soon as it ended ('With his
       surcease').
4   *his :* its.
       but this blow : this single blow.
5   *the be-all and the end-all :* all that is
       needed to end everything.
6   *upon this bank and shoal of time :* in
       this life. Macbeth imagines Time as a
       sandbank or shallow place ('shoal') in
       the sea of eternity.
7   *We'd jump the life to come :* I would
       take no notice of an eternal life after
       death (where there might be punish-
       ment for earthly sins).
7-8   *But . . . here :* for crimes like this,
       there is still judgement on earth.
8-10   *that . . . inventor :* we only teach
       others lessons in murder, and after
       the lessons have been learned, they
       come back to torment the man who
       first found them out.
10   *even-handed :* fair-minded.
11   *Commends :* prescribes.
       chalice : cup, especially one used in
       religious ceremonies.

Duncan   Give me your hand;
Conduct me to mine host: we love him highly,
30 And shall continue our graces towards him.
By your leave, hostess.   [*Exeunt*

Scene 7 *A room in Macbeth's castle*

*Music and torches. Servants, carrying
dishes for a feast, hurry across the stage.
Then enter* Macbeth

Macbeth
If it were done, when 'tis done, then 'twere well
It were done quickly; if th' assassination
Could trammel up the consequence, and catch,
With his surcease, success; that but this blow
5 Might be the be-all and the end-all—here,
But here, upon this bank and shoal of time,
We'd jump the life to come. But in these cases,
We still have judgement here; that we but teach
Bloody instructions, which, being taught, return
10 To plague the inventor; this even-handed justice
Commends the ingredients of our poison'd chalice
To our own lips. He's here in double trust:
First, as I am his kinsman and his subject,
Strong both against the deed; then, as his host,
15 Who should against his murderer shut the door,
Not bear the knife myself. Besides, this Duncan
Hath borne his faculties so meek, hath been
So clear in his great office, that his virtues
Will plead like angels, trumpet-tongu'd, against
20 The deep damnation of his taking-off;
And pity, like a naked new-born babe,
Striding the blast, or heaven's cherubin, hors'd
Upon the sightless couriers of the air,
Shall blow the horrid deed in every eye,
25 That tears shall drown the wind. I have no spur
To prick the sides of my intent, but only
Vaulting ambition, which o'er-leaps itself
And falls on the other.

Enter Lady Macbeth
                     How now! what news?

14   *Strong . . . deed.* Macbeth is both Duncan's kinsman and Duncan's subject, and these are two strong reasons to prevent this murder.

16–25   Duncan has been so fine a king that if he is murdered his virtues will have the powers of angels, and voices like trumpets, to cry out against the deed. Pity itself will be seen, as tender as a baby; and the cherubin (the highest order of angels) will ride on the winds and blow news of the crime into every man's eye, until so many tears will be shed that the winds themselves are drowned.

17   *borne . . . meek :* has been so humble in exercising the powers ('faculties') of a king.

18   *clear :* honourable.

20   *taking-off :* murder.

23   *sightless couriers :* invisible messengers (the winds).

25–8   Ambition is Macbeth's only motive, and his ambition is like a horse that tries to jump too high ('o'er-leaps itself') and falls on the other side of the fence.

32–5   Macbeth wants to enjoy the praises he has earned ('bought') as though they were new clothes. If he proceeds with the murder of Duncan he will lose men's good opinions of him, and it will be like throwing away his new clothes.

37   *green and pale :* sickly (as if the hope had a hangover).

39   *afeard :* afraid. Are you frightened to be in fact what you would like to be?

44   *wait upon :* follow.

45   *adage :* proverb. The saying is 'The cat would eat fish, but would not wet her feet'.
       Prithee : I pray thee.

46   *become :* be fitting for.

47   He who dares do more than is fitting for a man, is no man at all (he becomes a beast).

48   *break :* mention.

49   *durst :* dare (past tense).

Lady Macbeth
He has almost supp'd: why have you left the
  chamber?
  Macbeth
30 Hath he ask'd for me?
  Lady Macbeth   Know you not, he has?
  Macbeth
We will proceed no further in this business:
He hath honour'd me of late; and I have bought
Golden opinions from all sorts of people,
Which would be worn now in their newest gloss,
35 Not cast aside so soon.
  Lady Macbeth   Was the hope drunk,
Wherein you dress'd yourself? hath it slept since,
And wakes it now, to look so green and pale
At what it did so freely? From this time
Such I account thy love. Art thou afeard
40 To be the same in thine own act and valour
As thou art in desire? Wouldst thou have that
Which thou esteem'st the ornament of life,
And live a coward in thine own esteem,
Letting 'I dare not' wait upon 'I would',
45 Like the poor cat i' the adage?
  Macbeth   Prithee, peace.
I dare do all that may become a man;
Who dares do more, is none.
  Lady Macbeth   What beast was't, then,
That made you break this enterprise to me?
When you durst do it, then you were a man;
50 And, to be more than what you were, you would
Be so much more the man. Nor time nor place
Did then adhere, and yet you would make both:
They have made themselves, and that their fitness
  now
Does unmake you. I have given suck, and know
55 How tender 'tis to love the babe that milks me:
I would, while it was smiling in my face,
Have pluck'd my nipple from his boneless gums,
And dash'd the brains out, had I so sworn as you
Have done to this.
  Macbeth   If we should fail—
  Lady Macbeth   We fail?

51-4   When Macbeth first suggested the murder, neither time nor place was suitable, yet he would find a time and a place. Now both time and place are right, but because they are right he is afraid—made no longer a man.

60   *sticking-place.* The strings of a lute, or a modern guitar, are tightened and tuned by screwing the pegs to which they are fastened. Macbeth must screw up his courage like a guitar-string, until it is taut and has reached its 'sticking-place'.

64-7   I will overpower ('convince') his two attendants with wine and merry-making ('wassail') so that their memory, which guards the brain (according to Elizabethan anatomy) shall be a fog ('fume'), and the brain itself, the place where reason is received ('receipt of reason'), shall be no more than a chemist's distilling-flask ('limbeck').

68   *drenched :* soaked, drunken.

71   *spongy*—because they have soaked up so much wine, like sponges.

72   *quell :* kill, murder.

73   *mettle :* courage.

74   *receiv'd :* accepted.

77-8   Who will dare believe anything else, since we shall cry out with so much grief and noise?

79   *bend up :* make ready.

80   *corporal agent :* physical faculty.

81   *mock :* deceive.

60   But screw your courage to the sticking-place,
And we'll not fail. When Duncan is asleep,
Whereto the rather shall his day's hard journey
Soundly invite him, his two chamberlains
Will I with wine and wassail so convince,

65   That memory, the warder of the brain,
Shall be a fume, and the receipt of reason
A limbeck only; when in swinish sleep
Their drenched natures lie, as in a death,
What cannot you and I perform upon

70   The unguarded Duncan? what not put upon
His spongy officers, who shall bear the guilt
Of our great quell?

    Macbeth   Bring forth men-children only!
For thy undaunted mettle should compose
Nothing but males. Will it not be receiv'd,

75   When we have mark'd with blood those sleepy two
Of his own chamber, and us'd their very daggers,
That they have done 't?

    Lady Macbeth   Who dares receive it other,
As we shall make our griefs and clamour roar
Upon his death?

    Macbeth   I am settled, and bend up

80   Each corporal agent to this terrible feat.
Away, and mock the time with fairest show:
False face must hide what the false heart doth
    know.   *[Exeunt*

Act 2

Banquo and his son Fleance are on
their way to bed when they meet
Macbeth. He is nervously waiting the
signal to murder Duncan.

1   What time is it?

2   *is down :* has set.

3   *she :* the moon.

4   *husbandry :* economy

5   *Their candles :* the stars.
      that. Banquo perhaps gives his
cloak to Fleance.

6-9   Banquo feels heavy with sleep, as
though he is called to bed, yet he wants
to keep awake. He is afraid of the
thoughts that come when the body is
at rest.

14   *largess :* gifts.
      offices : servants' quarters.

15-16 *greets . . . hostess :* he addresses it
to your wife, as his most kind hostess.

16   *shut up :* ended the day.

Scene 1 *The courtyard of Macbeth's castle*

> *Enter* Banquo *and* Fleance, *with a*
> Servant *bearing a torch before them*

Banquo
How goes the night, boy?
      Fleance
The moon is down; I have not heard the clock.
      Banquo
And she goes down at twelve.
      Fleance   I take 't, 'tis later, sir.
      Banquo
Hold, take my sword. There's husbandry in
      heaven;

5 Their candles are all out. Take thee that too.
A heavy summons lies like lead upon me,
And yet I would not sleep: merciful powers,
Restrain in me the cursed thoughts that nature
Gives way to in repose.

> *Enter* Macbeth, *and a* Servant *with a torch*
>   Give me my sword.

10 Who's there?
      Macbeth
A friend.
      Banquo
What, sir! not yet at rest? The king's a-bed:
He hath been in unusual pleasure, and
Sent forth great largess to your offices.

15 This diamond he greets your wife withal,
By the name of most kind hostess; and shut up
In measureless content.

17-19 We were not prepared, and so we could not be as generous ('free') as we wished.

22   *an hour to serve :* a convenient time.

24   *At your kind'st leisure :* whenever you would be so kind as to spare the time.
25   If you will follow my advice, when the time comes.
26   *So :* provided that.
27   *augment :* increase.
28   *bosom franchis'd :* heart free from guilt.
  clear : loyal (to the king).
29   *be counsell'd :* listen to your advice.

36-7   *sensible . . . sight :* able to be felt as well as seen.

39   *heat-oppressed :* feverish.
40   *palpable :* touchable.

42   *marshall'st :* beckons.

Macbeth   Being unprepar'd,
Our will became the servant to defect,
Which else should free have wrought.
Banquo   All's well.
20 I dreamt last night of the three weird sisters:
To you they have show'd some truth.
Macbeth   I think not of them:
Yet, when we can entreat an hour to serve,
We would spend it in some words upon that
   business,
If you would grant the time.
Banquo   At your kind'st leisure.
Macbeth
25 If you shall cleave to my consent, when 'tis,
It shall make honour for you.
Banquo   So I lose none
In seeking to augment it, but still keep
My bosom franchis'd and allegiance clear,
I shall be counsell'd.
Macbeth   Good repose the while!
Banquo
30 Thanks, sir: the like to you.
                        [*Exeunt* Banquo *and* Fleance
Macbeth
Go bid thy mistress, when my drink is ready,
She strike upon the bell. Get thee to bed.
                              [*Exit* Servant
Is this a dagger which I see before me,
The handle toward my hand? Come, let me clutch
   thee:
35 I have thee not, and yet I see thee still.
Art thou not, fatal vision, sensible
To feeling as to sight? or art thou but
A dagger of the mind, a false creation,
Proceeding from the heat-oppressed brain?
40 I see thee yet, in form as palpable
As this which now I draw.
Thou marshall'st me the way that I was going;

And such an instrument I was to use.
Mine eyes are made the fools o' the other senses,
45 Or else worth all the rest: I see thee still;
And on thy blade and dudgeon gouts of blood,
Which was not so before. There's no such thing:
It is the bloody business which informs
Thus to mine eyes. Now o'er the one half-world
50 Nature seems dead, and wicked dreams abuse
The curtain'd sleep; witchcraft celebrates
Pale Hecate's offerings; and wither'd murder,
Alarum'd by his sentinel, the wolf,
Whose howl's his watch, thus with his stealthy pace,
55 With Tarquin's ravishing strides, toward his design
Moves like a ghost. Thou sure and firm-set earth,
Hear not my steps, which way they walk, for fear
Thy very stones prate of my whereabout,
And take the present horror from the time,
60 Which now suits with it. Whiles I threat, he lives:
Words to the heat of deeds too cold breath gives.
[*A bell rings*

I go, and it is done; the bell invites me.
Hear it not, Duncan; for it is a knell
That summons thee to heaven, or to hell.   [*Exit*

44-5   Either his eyes are foolish, compared to the other senses, or they are more trustworthy than all the rest.

46   *dudgeon*: hilt.
gouts: drops.

48-9   *informs Thus*: takes shape in this way.

49   *one half-world*: the hemisphere that is in darkness.

50   *abuse*: deceive.

51   *curtain'd*. The curtains are those of the four-poster bed, rather than window-curtains.
celebrates: performs the rites ('offerings').

52   *Hecate*: goddess of witches.

53   *Alarum'd*: woken up (as by a modern alarm-clock).
sentinel: guard, watchman.

54   *Whose howl's his watch*: the wolf's howl is like the cry of the night-watchman (who patrolled the streets of Elizabethan London).

55   *Tarquin*. Murder has been personified in line 52, and is now compared to the Roman Tarquin, who came in the night to rape ('ravish') his friend's wife, Lucrece. Shakespeare wrote a long poem, *The Rape of Lucrece*, on this subject.
design: aim.

58   *prate*: chatter.

59-60   *take . . . with it*: break the present horrible silence which is appropriate at this time.

60   *threat*: threaten.

61   Words are only breath, which is cold; deeds must be hot.

63   *knell*: funeral bell.

Act 2   scene 2

Lady Macbeth waits for her husband, who comes from Duncan's room with bloody hands.

1   *them :* Duncan's attendants.

2   *quench'd :* cooled, put out the fire.

4   *owl :* a bird of the night; the owl is compared to the man who rang the funeral ('fatal') bell outside the cells of prisoners condemned to die in Newgate prison.

5   *about it :* doing the deed.
6   *surfeited grooms :* drunken servants.
7   *possets :* hot drinks, 'nightcaps'.
8–9   Death and Life fight over the attendants to decide whether they should live or die.

12   *Confounds :* ruins.

16   *crickets :* chirping insects (which were thought by the Elizabethans to herald death).

21   *sorry :* miserable.

Scene 2 *The courtyard of Macbeth's castle*

Enter Lady Macbeth

Lady Macbeth

That which hath made them drunk hath made me bold,
What hath quench'd them hath given me fire. Hark! Peace!
It was the owl that shriek'd, the fatal bellman,
5 Which gives the stern'st good-night. He is about it:
The doors are open, and the surfeited grooms
Do mock their charge with snores: I have drugg'd their possets,
That death and nature do contend about them,
Whether they live or die.

Macbeth

[*Within*]   Who's there? what, ho!

Lady Macbeth

10 Alack! I am afraid they have awak'd,
And 'tis not done; the attempt and not the deed
Confounds us. Hark! I laid their daggers ready;
He could not miss 'em. Had he not resembled
My father as he slept, I had done't.

Enter Macbeth

My husband!

Macbeth

15 I have done the deed. Didst thou not hear a noise?

Lady Macbeth

I heard the owl scream and the crickets cry.
Did not you speak?

Macbeth   When?

Lady Macbeth   Now.

Macbeth   As I descended?

Lady Macbeth

Ay.

Macbeth

Hark!
20 Who lies i' the second chamber?

Lady Macbeth   Donalbain.

Macbeth

[*Looking at his hands*] This is a sorry sight.

Lady Macbeth

A foolish thought to say a sorry sight.

Macbeth
There's one did laugh in 's sleep, and one cried
'Murder!'
That they did wake each other: I stood and heard
them;
25 But they did say their prayers, and address'd them
Again to sleep.
Lady Macbeth   There are two lodg'd together.
Macbeth
One cried 'God bless us!', and 'Amen' the other,
As they had seen me with these hangman's hands.
Listening their fear, I could not say 'Amen',
30 When they did say 'God bless us!'
Lady Macbeth   Consider it not so deeply.
Macbeth
But wherefore could not I pronounce 'Amen'?
I had most need of blessing, and 'Amen'
Stuck in my throat.
Lady Macbeth These deeds must not be thought
After these ways; so, it will make us mad.
Macbeth
35 Methought I heard a voice cry 'Sleep no more!
Macbeth does murder sleep'—the innocent sleep,
Sleep that knits up the ravell'd sleave of care,
The death of each day's life, sore labour's bath,
Balm of hurt minds, great nature's second course,
40 Chief nourisher in life's feast—
Lady Macbeth   What do you mean?
Macbeth
Still it cried, 'Sleep no more!' to all the house:
'Glamis hath murder'd sleep, and therefore Cawdor
Shall sleep no more, Macbeth shall sleep no more!'
Lady Macbeth
Who was it that thus cried? Why, worthy thane,
45 You do unbend your noble strength to think
So brainsickly of things. Go, get some water,
And wash this filthy witness from your hand.
Why did you bring these daggers from the place?

25   *address'd them :* prepared
themselves.

26   *lodg'd :* housed.

28   *As :* as if.
hangman. The hangman drew the
entrails from his victims, and cut them
into quarters, after hanging them.
Therefore his hands were covered in
blood.
29   *Listening :* listening to.

37   *knits up :* smooths out, pieces
together.
ravell'd : tangled.
sleave : skein (of wool or silk).
39   *Balm :* soothing ointment.
39-40 *second course . . . feast.* The main
dish ('Chief nourisher') at a feast was
the 'second course'. Even today the
English eat soup or some small fish
dish before the main dish of meat.

45   *unbend :* relax (his strength had
previously been bent like a bow).
46   *brainsickly :* deliriously.
47   *witness :* evidence.

They must lie there: go, carry them, and smear
50 The sleepy grooms with blood.

Macbeth   I'll go no more:
I am afraid to think what I have done;
Look on 't again I dare not.

Lady Macbeth   Infirm of purpose!
Give me the daggers. The sleeping and the dead
Are but as pictures; 'tis the eye of childhood
55 That fears a painted devil. If he do bleed,
I'll gild the faces of the grooms withal;
For it must seem their guilt.

              [*Exit. Someone knocks at the gate*

     Macbeth   Whence is that knocking?
How is 't with me, when every noise appals me?
What hands are here! Ha! they pluck out mine eyes.
60 Will all great Neptune's ocean wash this blood
Clean from my hand? No, this my hand will rather
The multitudinous seas incarnadine,
Making the green one red.

         Enter Lady Macbeth

     Lady Macbeth
My hands are of your colour, but I shame
65 To wear a heart so white. [*Knocking*] I hear a
     knocking
At the south entry; retire we to our chamber;
A little water clears us of this deed;
How easy is it, then! Your constancy
Hath left you unattended. [*Knocking*] Hark! more
     knocking.
70 Get on your night-gown, lest occasion call us,
And show us to be watchers. Be not lost
So poorly in your thoughts.

     Macbeth
To know my deed 'twere best not know myself.

                [*Knocking*
Wake Duncan with thy knocking! I would thou
     couldst!   [*Exeunt*

---

55   *a painted devil :* a picture of a devil.

57   *guilt.* Lady Macbeth makes a cruel pun here on *guilt* and *gilt.*

59   *they pluck out mine eyes.* Macbeth's eyes are almost falling out of his head at the sight of his bloody hands.

62   *multitudinous :* very great in number.
incarnadine : dye scarlet (see A play for the king, p. vi).

68-9   Your strength of mind has deserted you.

70   *lest occasion call us :* in case there is need to call for us.

71   *watchers :* still awake, not in bed.

72   *poorly :* feebly.

73   If I must recognize what I have done, it would be better that I did not recognize myself (because the deed is damnable, and he would have to condemn himself).

74   *I would thou couldst :* I wish you could.

Act 2   scene 3

All is discovered. The Porter is roused
from his drunken sleep by Macduff
and Lennox. They go to call upon the
king but find that he has been
murdered. Macbeth panics and kills
Duncan's attendants, explaining that
he did this from a sense of outraged
loyalty and grief. Duncan's two sons
are afraid for their own safety, and slip
away secretly.

2   *have old* : have plenty of.
4   *Beelzebub* : one of the chief devils.
4-5   *farmer . . . plenty* : the farmer had
hoarded his corn, hoping for a famine
when the price of corn would rise;
hearing that the harvests were good
(and the price would fall) he hanged
himself.
6   *time-server* : one who changes his
opinions to suit the times.
        napkins : handkerchiefs.
8   *the other devil*. The Porter cannot
remember the name of another devil.
9   *equivocator* : double-dealer, one
who avoids telling the truth without
actually telling a lie.
        the scales : the scales held by the
statue of Justice.
13-14 *English tailor . . . French hose* : the

Scene 3 *The courtyard of Macbeth's castle*

Knocking. Enter a Porter

Porter

Here's a knocking, indeed! If a man were porter of
hell-gate, he should have old turning the key.
[*Knocking*] Knock, knock, knock! Who's there,
i' the name of Beelzebub? Here's a farmer that
5 hanged himself on the expectation of plenty : come in
time-server; have napkins enough about you; here
you'll sweat for 't. [*Knocking*] Knock, knock! Who's
there, i' the other devil's name! Faith, here's an
equivocator, that could swear in both the scales
10 against either scale; who committed treason enough
for God's sake, yet could not equivocate to heaven :
O! come in, equivocator. [*Knocking*] Knock, knock,
knock! Who's there? Faith, here's an English
tailor come hither for stealing out of a French hose :
15 come in, tailor; here you may roast your goose.
[*Knocking*] Knock, knock; never at quiet! What
are you? But this place is too cold for hell. I'll
devil-porter it no further: I had thought to have
let in some of all professions, that go the primrose
20 way to the everlasting bonfire. [*Knocking*] Anon,
anon! I pray you, remember the porter.

[*Opens the gate*

tailor had tried to steal material when he was making tight-fitting breeches ('French hose'), and so made them too tight, and was caught.

15   *roast your goose :* the 'goose' was a tailor's flat-iron.

19-20   *primrose way :* easy path; the 'primrose' is a delicate, yellow, spring flower.

20   *everlasting bonfire :* hell.

20-1   *Anon, anon :* I'm coming.

21   *remember the porter :* tip the porter for opening the gate.

23   *lie so late :* sleep so late.

24   *carousing :* drinking.
    second cock : second cock-crow, well after dawn.

27   *Marry :* by the Virgin Mary (but the oath was so common that it means no more than 'indeed').
    nose-painting : it makes the nose red.

28-36   'Drink is a double-dealer ("equivocator") so far as lechery is concerned, because it makes a man feel virile, but at the same time renders him impotent ("mars him").' The Porter repeats this idea, in different words, three times, then concludes that drink cheats a man with a dream, lies to him (and makes him lie down), and leaves him.

38   *i' the very throat :* a direct lie (not an equivocation).
    on me : of me.

39   *requited :* paid him back.

40   *he took up my legs :* I fell down.

41   *made a shift :* contrived.
    to cast : to throw him down (by urinating).

42   *stirring :* awake.

46   *timely :* early.

47   *slipp'd the hour :* missed the time.

Enter Macduff *and* Lennox

Macduff
Was it so late, friend, ere you went to bed, that you do lie so late?

Porter
Faith, sir, we were carousing till the second cock;
25 and drink, sir, is a great provoker of three things.

Macduff
What three things does drink especially provoke?

Porter
Marry, sir, nose-painting, sleep, and urine. Lechery, sir, it provokes, and unprovokes: it provokes the desire, but it takes away the per-
30 formance. Therefore, much drink may be said to be an equivocator with lechery: it makes him, and it mars him; it sets him on, and it takes him off; it persuades him, and disheartens him; makes him stand to, and not stand to: in conclusion,
35 equivocates him in a sleep, and, giving him the lie, leaves him.

Macduff
I believe drink gave thee the lie last night.

Porter
That it did, sir; i' the very throat on me: but I requited him for his lie, and (I think) being too
40 strong for him, though he took up my legs some-time, yet I made a shift to cast him.

Macduff
Is thy master stirring?

Enter Macbeth
Our knocking has awak'd him; here he comes.

Lennox
Good morrow, noble sir.

Macbeth   Good morrow, both.

Macduff
45 Is the king stirring, worthy thane?

Macbeth   Not yet.

Macduff
He did command me to call timely on him: I have almost slipp'd the hour.

Macbeth   I'll bring you to him.

50 Work that we enjoy cures ('physics')
any trouble ('pain') that it causes us.

52 *limited*: appointed.

58 *dire combustion*: terrible confusion.
59 *hatch'd*: born (as chickens are
'hatched' from eggs).
woeful time. Lennox refers to the
war with Norway, but his words are
unintentionally apt to describe the
events of the past night.
obscure bird: owl, the bird of
darkness (obscurity).
60 *livelong*: entire.
62-3 In all my young life I cannot
remember a night like this.

66 *Confusion*: chaos.
67 *sacrilegious*: unholy.
ope: open.
68 *anointed*. When he was crowned
king, Duncan would have been
anointed with holy oil, to signify that
he was God's deputy on earth.

Macduff
I know this is a joyful trouble to you;
But yet 'tis one.
Macbeth
50 The labour we delight in physics pain.
This is the door.
Macduff   I'll make so bold to call,
For 'tis my limited service.   [*Exit*
Lennox
Goes the king hence to-day?
Macbeth   He does: he did appoint so.
Lennox
The night has been unruly: where we lay,
55 Our chimneys were blown down; and, as they say,
Lamentings heard i' the air; strange screams of death,
And prophesying with accents terrible
Of dire combustion and confus'd events
New hatch'd to the woeful time. The obscure bird
60 Clamour'd the livelong night: some say the earth
Was feverous and did shake.
Macbeth   'Twas a rough night.
Lennox
My young remembrance cannot parallel
A fellow to it.

Re-enter Macduff

Macduff
O horror! horror! horror! Tongue nor heart
65 Cannot conceive nor name thee!
Macbeth }
Lennox }   What's the matter?
Macduff
Confusion now hath made his masterpiece!
Most sacrilegious murder hath broke ope
The Lord's anointed temple, and stole thence
The life o' the building!
Macbeth
70 What is 't you say? the life?
Lennox
Mean you his majesty?

73   *Gorgon*. In Greek mythology the Gorgon Medusa, a monster with snakes instead of hair, turned every man to stone who looked on her. The sight of Duncan's murdered body will have the same effect.

77-81   Macduff calls on everyone to wake from sleep, which is an imitation ('counterfeit') of death, to look at the real thing, and to rise up like ghosts ('sprites') from their graves to come face to face ('countenance') with this horror, as terrible as a picture of the Last Judgement ('great doom').

77   *downy :* comfortable (because their pillows would be stuffed with 'down', the soft feathers of ducks and geese).

83   *calls to parley :* summons to a discussion.

86-7   To repeat this matter to a woman would kill her as she heard it.

92   *before this chance :* before this happened.

94   *nothing serious in mortality :* nothing important in life.

95   *toys :* trifles.

96-7   Macbeth compares the earth to a wine-cellar ('vault') from which the best wine has been drawn, so that it can now boast ('brag') only of the dregs ('lees').

Macduff
Approach the chamber, and destroy your sight
With a new Gorgon: do not bid me speak;
See, and then speak yourselves.
                    [*Exeunt* Macbeth *and* Lennox
                              Awake! awake!
75 Ring the alarum-bell. Murder and treason!
Banquo and Donalbain! Malcolm, awake!
Shake off this downy sleep, death's counterfeit,
And look on death itself! Up, up, and see
The great doom's image! Malcolm! Banquo!
80 As from your graves rise up, and walk like sprites,
To countenance this horror! Ring the bell.
                                   [*Bell rings*

            Enter Lady Macbeth
      Lady Macbeth
What's the business,
That such a hideous trumpet calls to parley
The sleepers of the house? Speak, speak!
      Macduff   O gentle lady!
85 'Tis not for you to hear what I can speak;
The repetition in a woman's ear
Would murder as it fell.

            Enter Banquo
                              O Banquo! Banquo!
Our royal master's murder'd!
      Lady Macbeth   Woe, alas!
What! in our house?
      Banquo   Too cruel anywhere.
90 Dear Duff, I prithee, contradict thyself,
And say it is not so.

            Enter Macbeth *and* Lennox
      Macbeth
Had I but died an hour before this chance,
I had liv'd a blessed time; for, from this instant,
There 's nothing serious in mortality,
95 All is but toys; renown and grace is dead,
The wine of life is drawn, and the mere lees
Is left this vault to brag of.

Enter Malcolm *and* Donalbain

Donalbain

What is amiss?

Macbeth   You are, and do not know 't:

The spring, the head, the fountain of your blood

100 Is stopp'd; the very source of it is stopp'd.

Macduff

Your royal father's murder'd.

Malcolm   O! by whom?

Lennox

Those of his chamber, as it seem'd, had done 't:

Their hands and faces were all badg'd with blood;

So were their daggers, which unwip'd we found

105 Upon their pillows: they star'd, and were distracted;

No man's life was to be trusted with them.

Macbeth

O yet I do repent me of my fury,

That I did kill them.

Macduff   Wherefore did you so?

Macbeth

Who can be wise, amaz'd, temperate and furious,

110 Loyal and neutral, in a moment? No man.

The expedition of my violent love

Outran the pauser, reason. Here lay Duncan,

His silver skin lac'd with his golden blood;

And his gash'd stabs look'd like a breach in nature

115 For ruin's wasteful entrance: there, the murderers,

Steep'd in the colours of their trade, their daggers

Unmannerly breech'd with gore: who could refrain,

That had a heart to love, and in that heart

Courage to make 's love known?

Lady Macbeth   Help me hence, ho!

Macduff

120 Look to the lady.

Malcolm

[*Aside to* Donalbain] Why do we hold our tongues,

That most may claim this argument for ours?

Donalbain

[*Aside to* Malcolm] What should be spoken

Here where our fate, hid in an auger-hole,

May rush and seize us? Let's away: our tears

125 Are not yet brew'd.

---

98   *amiss*: wrong.

103   *badg'd*: wearing the badges of their
        profession (as murderers).

111   *expedition*: speed.

112   *pauser*: delayer, that which makes
        one stop and think.

114-15 Duncan's wounds were like
        openings in his body where destruction
        ('ruin') had forced an entrance to lay
        waste his life.

116   Macbeth repeats Lennox's
        thought (line 103), that the servants
        were wearing the coloured uniforms of
        their trade as murderers.
        steep'd: dyed.

117   *Unmannerly*: indecently.
        breech'd: clothed (in breeches).
        refrain: stop himself from acting.

121   *argument*: topic of discussion.

122-4   What can we say here, where our
        fate (death) may be hiding in some tiny
        hole, ready to rush upon and seize us?
        (An auger is a sharp-pointed tool for
        boring holes in wood.)

125   *brew'd*: ready to flow (tea is said
        to be 'brewed' when it is ready to
        drink).

126   *Upon the foot of motion :* ready to move—to express itself either in words or in actions.
127-8   When we have dressed our weak (because unclothed) bodies, so that we don't catch cold from exposure.
129   *question :* investigate.
130   *scruples :* doubts.
131   *In the great hand of God :* in God's great protection.
132   *undivulg'd pretence :* hidden design.

134   *briefly :* quickly.
      manly readiness : proper clothing (and also, perhaps, determination).

136   *consort :* mix.
137   *office :* duty.
138   *easy :* easily.

141-2   The closer we are in relationship ('in blood') to the king, the more likely we are to be murdered.
142   *shaft :* arrow.
143   *lighted :* alighted, found its mark.
144   *avoid the aim :* keep out of its way.
145   *dainty of leave-taking :* fussy about saying a formal goodbye.
146   *shift away :* steal away.
146-7   It is a justifiable theft, to steal (oneself) away from a place where there is no mercy.

Malcolm
[*Aside to* Donalbain] Nor our strong sorrow
Upon the foot of motion.
    Banquo   Look to the lady:
                 [Lady Macbeth *is carried out*
And when we have our naked frailties hid,
That suffer in exposure, let us meet,
And question this most bloody piece of work,
130 To know it further. Fears and scruples shake us:
In the great hand of God I stand, and thence
Against the undivulg'd pretence I fight
Of treasonous malice.
    Macduff   And so do I.
    All   So all.
    Macbeth
Let's briefly put on manly readiness,
135 And meet i' the hall together.
    All   Well contented.
          [*Exeunt all but* Malcolm *and* Donalbain
    Malcolm
What will you do? Let's not consort with them:
To show an unfelt sorrow is an office
Which the false man does easy. I'll to England.
    Donalbain
To Ireland, I; our separated fortune
140 Shall keep us both the safer: where we are,
There's daggers in men's smiles: the near in blood,
The nearer bloody.
    Malcolm   This murderous shaft that's shot
Hath not yet lighted, and our safest way
Is to avoid the aim: therefore, to horse;
145 And let us not be dainty of leave-taking,
But shift away: there's warrant in that theft
Which steals itself when there's no mercy left.
                 [*Exeunt*

Act 2   scene 4

Ross and an Old Man discuss the unnatural events that occurred on the night of Duncan's murder. They learn from Macduff that the king's two sons have fled, and that because of this they are suspected of having bribed their father's servants to murder him. Macduff also tells them that Macbeth has been chosen as king, and that he has gone to Scone for the coronation.

3   *sore :* strange.
4   *trifled former knowings :* made all that I have known before seem trivial.
5   *troubled :* angered.
7   *strangles the travelling lamp :* chokes the sun (with clouds).
8   *predominance :* superior power.
9   *entomb :* bury.

12   *falcon :* a bird of prey, beautiful and fierce.
     pride of place : highest point of the falcon's flight.
13   *mousing :* that catches mice.
     hawk'd : pounced upon from the air, as a hawk (a bird even more powerful than the falcon) catches its prey.

15   *minions of their race :* the best (most favoured) of their breed.
16   *broke their stalls :* broke out of their stables.
17   *Contending 'gainst obedience :* fighting against the training that made them obedient.

Scene 4 *Outside Macbeth's castle*

Enter Ross *and an* Old Man

Old Man
Threescore and ten I can remember well;
Within the volume of which time I have seen
Hours dreadful and things strange, but this sore night
Hath trifled former knowings.
Ross   Ah good father,
5 Thou seest the heavens, as troubled with man's act,
Threaten his bloody stage: by the clock 'tis day,
And yet dark night strangles the travelling lamp.
Is 't night's predominance, or the day's shame,
That darkness does the face of earth entomb,
10 When living light should kiss it?
Old Man   'Tis unnatural,
Even like the deed that's done. On Tuesday last,
A falcon, towering in her pride of place,
Was by a mousing owl hawk'd at and kill'd.
Ross
And Duncan's horses—a thing most strange and certain—
15 Beauteous and swift, the minions of their race,
Turn'd wild in nature, broke their stalls, flung out,
Contending 'gainst obedience, as they would
Make war with mankind.
Old Man   'Tis said they ate each other.
Ross
They did so, to the amazement of mine eyes,
20 That look'd upon 't. Here comes the good Macduff.

Enter Macduff

How goes the world, sir, now?

Macduff   Why, see you not?

Ross

Is 't known who did this more than bloody deed?

Macduff

Those that Macbeth hath slain.

Ross   Alas, the day!

What good could they pretend?

Macduff   They were suborn'd.

25 Malcolm and Donalbain, the king's two sons,
Are stol'n away and fled, which puts upon them
Suspicion of the deed.

Ross   'Gainst nature still!

Thriftless ambition, that wilt ravin up
Thine own life's means! Then 'tis most like

30 The sovereignty will fall upon Macbeth.

Macduff

He is already nam'd, and gone to Scone
To be invested.

Ross   Where is Duncan's body?

Macduff

Carried to Colmekill,
The sacred storehouse of his predecessors

35 And guardian of their bones.

Ross   Will you to Scone?

Macduff

No, cousin, I'll to Fife.

Ross   Well, I will thither.

Macduff

Well, may you see things well done there: adieu!
Lest our old robes sit easier than our new!

Ross

Farewell, father.

Old Man

40 God's benison go with you; and with those
That would make good of bad, and friends of foes!

[*Exeunt*

24   *What . . . pretend :* what good did they
     think it would do them?
     suborn'd : bribed.

27   *still :* again.
28   *ravin up :* devour.
29   *Thine own life's means :* that which
     is necessary to give you life.
30   *sovereignty :* kingship.

31   *nam'd :* elected.
     Scone : at one time the capital of
     Scotland. (The Stone of Scone, on
     which Scottish kings were crowned, is
     now kept in Westminster Abbey, and
     it is used in British coronation
     ceremonies.)
32   *invested :* made king (at a ceremony
     where he receives the symbols of
     royalty—see illustration, p. 65).

38   *sit :* fit.

40   *benison :* blessing.

Act 3

Act 3   scene 1

Banquo suspects Macbeth, but he still
hopes that the witches' prophecy may
also come true for him. He promises
Macbeth that he will return in time for
the feast, and then leaves Macbeth
alone on the stage. Macbeth reveals his
inmost thoughts to us, before the
Murderers are brought in, and a new
plot is started.

4   The crown would not be passed on to
Macbeth's descendants.

7   *shine :* show favour (as the sun shines).

8   *verities . . . good :* truths which have
been proved in your case.

9   *my oracles :* prophets for me.

14 *solemn supper :* formal dinner.

16 *to the which :* to which command.

17 *indissoluble :* which cannot be broken.

18 *knit :* bound.

Scene 1 *Forres. A room in the palace*

Enter Banquo

Banquo

Thou hast it now: King, Cawdor, Glamis, all,
As the weird women promis'd; and, I fear,
Thou play'dst most foully for 't; yet it was said
It should not stand in thy posterity,
5 But that myself should be the root and father
Of many kings. If there come truth from them—
As upon thee, Macbeth, their speeches shine—
Why, by the verities on thee made good,
May they not be my oracles as well,
10 And set me up in hope? But, hush! no more.

A trumpet sounds. Enter Macbeth, *as king;*
Lady Macbeth, *as queen;* Lennox, Ross,
Lords, Ladies, *and* Attendants

Macbeth

Here's our chief guest.

Lady Macbeth   If he had been forgotten,
It had been as a gap in our great feast,
And all-thing unbecoming.

Macbeth

To-night we hold a solemn supper, sir,
15 And I'll request your presence.

Banquo   Let your highness
Command upon me; to the which my duties
Are with a most indissoluble tie
For ever knit.

Macbeth
Ride you this afternoon?
Banquo
20 Ay, my good lord.
Macbeth
We should have else desir'd your good advice—
Which still hath been both grave and prosperous—
In this day's council; but we'll take to-morrow.
Is 't far you ride?
Banquo
25 As far, my lord, as will fill up the time
'Twixt this and supper; go not my horse the better,
I must become a borrower of the night
For a dark hour or twain.
Macbeth   Fail not our feast.
Banquo
My lord, I will not.
Macbeth
30 We hear our bloody cousins are bestow'd
In England and in Ireland, not confessing
Their cruel parricide, filling their hearers
With strange invention; but of that to-morrow,
When, therewithal, we shall have cause of state
35 Craving us jointly. Hie you to horse; adieu
Till you return at night. Goes Fleance with you?
Banquo
Ay, my good lord: our time does call upon 's.
Macbeth
I wish your horses swift and sure of foot;
And so I do commend you to their backs.
40 Farewell.   [*Exit* Banquo
Let every man be master of his time
Till seven at night; to make society
The sweeter welcome, we will keep ourself
Till supper-time alone; while then, God be with
    you!
                    [*Exeunt all but* Macbeth *and an* Attendant
45 Sirrah, a word with you. Attend those men
Our pleasure?
Attendant
They are, my lord, without the palace gate.

22   *still :* always.
    grave : serious.
    prosperous : profitable.

26   *this :* this time.
26-8 If my horse does not go faster than
    I expect, I shall have to use one or two
    ('twain') hours of darkness from the
    night.

30   *bloody :* stained with the blood of
    Duncan.
    bestow'd : settled.

33   *strange invention :* strange tales
    which they have invented.
33-5 We will talk more of that tomorrow,
    when there will also be affairs of state,
    that demand the attention of both of us.

37   *our time does call upon 's :* it is time
    for us to go.

41   *master of his time :* use his time as
    he wishes.

47   *without :* outside.

48-9	It is nothing to be as I am now (i.e. king); I must be king in safety.
50	*stick deep*: are deeply rooted.
	royalty of nature: nobility of character.
51	*that . . . fear'd*: that which Macbeth ought to be afraid of.
52	*temper*: courage, spirit.
55	*being*: existence.
56-7	Macbeth's guiding spirit ('genius') is made timid by Banquo's—just as the Roman Mark Antony's spirit was said (by Plutarch) to be subdued by Julius Caesar's.
57	*chid*: reproached.
61-2	The witches gave Macbeth a crown and sceptre, but without the promise that his descendants would inherit them.
62	*gripe*: grasp.
63	*an unlineal hand*: a hand that does not belong to any of my descendants.
65	*fil'd*: defiled.
67	*rancours*: bitternesses.
68	*eternal jewel*: i.e. his immortal soul.
69	*common enemy of man*: i.e. Satan, who is the enemy of all men in general (in 'common'), not of one man in particular.
71-2	Macbeth calls upon Fate to come as a knight to tournament ('the list') to fight as a champion against him, to the death ('utterance' = utmost).
77	*he*: i.e. Banquo.
78	*under fortune*: below what you deserved.
80	*pass'd in probation*: demonstrated to you.
81	*borne in hand*: deceived.
	cross'd: thwarted.
	instruments: the means used.

Macbeth
Bring them before us. [*Exit* Attendant] To be thus
  is nothing;
But to be safely thus. Our fears in Banquo
50 Stick deep, and in his royalty of nature
Reigns that which would be fear'd: 'tis much he
  dares,
And, to that dauntless temper of his mind,
He hath a wisdom that doth guide his valour
To act in safety. There is none but he
55 Whose being I do fear; and under him
My genius is rebuk'd, as, it is said,
Mark Antony's was by Caesar. He chid the sisters
When first they put the name of king upon me,
And bade them speak to him; then, prophet-like,
60 They hail'd him father to a line of kings.
Upon my head they plac'd a fruitless crown,
And put a barren sceptre in my gripe,
Thence to be wrench'd with an unlineal hand,
No son of mine succeeding. If 't be so,
65 For Banquo's issue have I fil'd my mind;
For them the gracious Duncan have I murder'd;
Put rancours in the vessel of my peace
Only for them; and mine eternal jewel
Given to the common enemy of man,
70 To make them kings, the seed of Banquo kings!
Rather than so, come fate into the list,
And champion me to th' utterance! Who's there?

Enter Attendant, *with two* Murderers
Now go to the door, and stay there till we call.
                              [*Exit* Attendant
Was it not yesterday we spoke together?
First Murderer
75 It was, so please your highness.
Macbeth   Well then, now
Have you consider'd of my speeches? Know
That it was he, in the times past, which held you
So under fortune, which you thought had been
Our innocent self. This I made good to you
80 In our last conference, pass'd in probation with
  you,
How you were borne in hand, how cross'd, the
  instruments,

82   *wrought* : worked.

83   *half a soul* : a half-wit.
       notion craz'd : the mind of a
madman.

86–8   Is patience so much the strongest
of all your qualities that you will
endure this?

88   *gospell'd* : filled with the teaching
of the Christian Gospels.

89   *this good man.* Macbeth is being
ironic.
       issue : descendants.

91   *yours* : your descendants.

92–101   In the general list of natural
beings they are classified as 'men', just
as there are different breeds of dog
which are all included under 'dog'.
But the really valuable list ('file') is
that which notes the precise qualities
of every animal, according to its
natural gifts. This list which notes
special qualities ('Particular addition')
is distinct from the list ('bill') that
counts them all the same. This is true
of men, just as it is of dogs.

94   *Shoughs* : shaggy dogs.
       water-rugs : rough-haired water
dogs.
       demi-wolves : cross-breeds: half-
wolf, half-dog.
       clept : called.

97   *housekeeper* : guard-dog.

102   *station* : position.

104–5   I will tell you secretly ('in your
bosoms') of a plan which, when it is
carried out, will remove your enemy.

106   Fasten you firmly to my heart
and love.

107–8   Macbeth can only be sick whilst
Banquo is alive, but if Banquo were
dead, he would be perfectly healthy.

109   *buffets* : misfortunes.

110   *incens'd* : angered.

112   *tugg'd with* : dragged about by.

113–14   I would risk my life on any
gamble, where I could either improve
it or lose it.

Who wrought with them, and all things else that
     might
To half a soul and to a notion craz'd
Say, 'Thus did Banquo.'
> **First Murderer**   You made it known to us.
> **Macbeth**

85   I did so; and went further, which is now
Our point of second meeting. Do you find
Your patience so predominant in your nature
That you can let this go? Are you so gospell'd
To pray for this good man and for his issue,

90   Whose heavy hand hath bow'd you to the grave
And beggar'd yours for ever?
> **First Murderer**   We are men, my liege.
> **Macbeth**

Ay, in the catalogue ye go for men;
As hounds and greyhounds, mongrels, spaniels,
     curs,
Shoughs, water-rugs, and demi-wolves, are clept

95   All by the name of dogs: the valu'd file
Distinguishes the swift, the slow, the subtle,
The housekeeper, the hunter, every one
According to the gift which bounteous nature
Hath in him clos'd; whereby he does receive

100   Particular addition, from the bill
That writes them all alike: and so of men.
Now, if you have a station in the file,
Not i' the worst rank of manhood, say it;
And I will put that business in your bosoms,

105   Whose execution takes your enemy off,
Grapples you to the heart and love of us,
Who wear our health but sickly in his life,
Which in his death were perfect.
> **Second Murderer**   I am one, my liege,

Whom the vile blows and buffets of the world

110   Have so incens'd that I am reckless what
I do to spite the world.
> **First Murderer**   And I another,

So weary with disasters, tugg'd with fortune,
That I would set my life on any chance,
To mend it or be rid on 't.

Macbeth   Both of you
115 Know Banquo was your enemy.
           Second Murderer   True, my lord.
           Macbeth
     So is he mine; and in such bloody distance
     That every minute of his being thrusts
     Against my near'st of life: and though I could
     With bare-fac'd power sweep him from my sight
120 And bid my will avouch it, yet I must not,
     For certain friends that are both his and mine,
     Whose loves I may not drop, but wail his fall
     Who I myself struck down; and thence it is
     That I to your assistance do make love,
125 Masking the business from the common eye
     For sundry weighty reasons.
           Second Murderer   We shall, my lord,
     Perform what you command us.
           First Murderer   Though our lives—
           Macbeth
     Your spirits shine through you. Within this hour
                 at most
     I will advise you where to plant yourselves,
130 Acquaint you with the perfect spy o' the time,
     The moment on 't; for 't must be done to-night,
     And something from the palace; always thought
     That I require a clearness: and with him—
     To leave no rubs nor botches in the work—
135 Fleance his son, that keeps him company,
     Whose absence is no less material to me
     Than is his father's, must embrace the fate
     Of that dark hour. Resolve yourselves apart;
     I'll come to you anon.
           Second Murderer We are resolv'd, my lord.
           Macbeth
140 I'll call upon you straight: abide within.
                                  [*Exeunt* Murderers
     It is concluded: Banquo, thy soul's flight,
     If it find heaven, must find it out to-night.   [*Exit*

---

116 *bloody distance*: deadly distance ('distance' is a technical term in fencing for the space between two fighters).
117 *thrusts*: i.e. like a fencer's sword.
118 *near'st of life*: vital parts.
119 *bare-fac'd*: openly; Macbeth as king has power to kill Banquo without giving any excuse for his action.
120 *bid my will avouch it*: say I did it because I wanted to.
121 *For*: because.
122 *may not drop*: must not lose.
       but wail: instead I must lament.
124 *make love*: make advances.
125 *common eye*: public gaze.
126 *sundry*: various.

129 *plant*: hide.
130 *perfect spy o' the time*: the best time that I can see for the murder.
132 *something from*: at a distance from.
       always thought: always have it in your mind.
133 *I require a clearness*: I want to be free from suspicion.
134 *rubs*: mistakes.
       botches: bungling.
136 *absence*: death.
       material: important.
138 *Resolve yourselves apart*: make up your minds in private.
139 *anon*: immediately
140 *straight*: straight away, at once.

Act 3   scene 2
Macbeth and his wife are both worried.
He tells her that he is going to take
some action, but he will not tell her
what it is.

3-4   I will wait until he has time to
speak to me.

4-7   We have gained nothing, and lost
everything, when we are not satisfied
by getting what we wanted. It is better
to be that which we kill than, as a
result of killing, live in an insecure
('doubtful') pleasure.

9-11   Having depressing imagination for
·your companion, and living with those
thoughts that should have died when
the subject of them (i.e. Duncan) was
killed.

12   *without regard :* ignored.

13-15   Macbeth feels that although he is
evil, his evilness is feeble ('poor'), and
it is in danger now, just as it was
before the death of Duncan, from
righteousness, which Macbeth sees as
a snake which has been wounded
('scorch'd') but which will heal up
('close').

16   *frame of things :* structure of
creation.
disjoint : collapse.
both the worlds : heaven and earth.

21   *on :* in.

25   *foreign levy :* armies gathered
(levied) abroad.

Scene 2 *Another room in the palace*

Enter Lady Macbeth *and a* Servant

Lady Macbeth
Is Banquo gone from court?
Servant
Ay, madam, but returns again to-night.
Lady Macbeth
Say to the king, I would attend his leisure
For a few words.
Servant   Madam, I will.   [*Exit*
Lady Macbeth   Nought's had, all's spent,
5 Where our desire is got without content:
'Tis safer to be that which we destroy
Than by destruction dwell in doubtful joy.

Enter Macbeth

How now, my lord! why do you keep alone,
Of sorriest fancies your companions making,
10 Using those thoughts which should indeed have
died
With them they think on? Things without all
remedy
Should be without regard: what's done is done.
Macbeth
We have scorch'd the snake, not kill'd it:
She'll close and be herself, whilst our poor malice
15 Remains in danger of her former tooth.
But let the frame of things disjoint, both the worlds
suffer,
Ere we will eat our meal in fear, and sleep
In the affliction of these terrible dreams
That shake us nightly. Better be with the dead,
20 Whom we, to gain our peace, have sent to peace,
Than on the torture of the mind to lie
In restless ecstasy. Duncan is in his grave;
After life's fitful fever he sleeps well;
Treason has done his worst: nor steel, nor poison,
25 Malice domestic, foreign levy, nothing

27 *sleek o'er* : smooth down.

30 Remember Banquo (because she will remember what has been prophesied to him).

31 *Present him eminence* : pay him great respect.

32-3 As long as we are unsafe, we must wash our titles in flattery as though it were a stream (so that the titles of 'king' and 'queen' would seem to be clean and honourable).

34 *vizards* : masks, especially the part of the helmet that covers the face.

38 Nature (or Life) does not hold an eternal copyright on Banquo and Fleance (so that they can never die).

39 *they are assailable* : they can be attacked.

40 *jocund* : joyful.
    bat. The bat is like a mouse with wings, which flies only in the dark; it often lives in old churches with lonely 'cloisters'.

41 *Hecate* : goddess of witches.

42 *beetle.* The beetle flies at night (when men are sleepy—'drowsy'), and makes a humming noise which seems like a curfew bell ('night's . . . peal') rung when men are 'yawning'.

44 *dreadful note* : terrible to hear of.

45 *chuck.* A term of endearment, still used in England in parts of the Midlands.

46 *seeling* : blinding. This is a technical term from hunting; a falcon's eyes were 'seeled' when the eyelids were sewn with thread to make the bird helpless so that it would become tame.

49 *that great bond* : Banquo's life, which Macbeth thinks of as a legal document.

Can touch him further.

Lady Macbeth   Come on;
Gentle my lord, sleek o'er your rugged looks;
Be bright and jovial among your guests to-night.

Macbeth
So shall I, love; and so, I pray, be you.

30 Let your remembrance apply to Banquo;
Present him eminence, both with eye and tongue:
Unsafe the while, that we
Must lave our honours in these flattering streams,
And make our faces vizards to our hearts,

35 Disguising what they are.

Lady Macbeth   You must leave this.

Macbeth
O full of scorpions is my mind, dear wife;
Thou know'st that Banquo and his Fleance lives.

Lady Macbeth
But in them nature's copy's not eterne.

Macbeth
There's comfort yet; they are assailable;

40 Then be thou jocund. Ere the bat hath flown
His cloister'd flight, ere to black Hecate's summons
The shard-born beetle with his drowsy hums
Hath rung night's yawning peal, there shall be done
A deed of dreadful note.

Lady Macbeth   What's to be done?

Macbeth

45 Be innocent of the knowledge, dearest chuck,
Till thou applaud the deed. Come, seeling night,
Scarf up the tender eye of pitiful day,
And with thy bloody and invisible hand
Cancel and tear to pieces that great bond

50   *keeps me pale :* keeps me fenced in. The 'pale' was the boundary dividing one country's land from another's.

     crow : a large and ugly black bird, similar to the 'rook'.

53   The wicked beings that work in the night become alert in hunting their prey.

55   Deeds that are started with evil grow stronger with more evil.

Act 3   scene 3

A third murderer appears unexpectedly, and helps to murder Banquo.

2   *He . . . mistrust :* there is no need for him to mistrust us.

2-3   *delivers Our offices :* tells us our duties.

4   *To the direction just :* to the last detail.

6   *lated :* belated.

7   *To . . . inn :* to get to the inn in time (before dark).

8   *subject of our watch :* the man we are watching for.

10   *note of expectation :* the list of guests expected (for the banquet).

11   *go about :* go a long way round. After a long journey the horses would be sweating, and it would be necessary for the grooms (called by Banquo in line 9) to walk with them until they were cool.

---

50 Which keeps me pale! Light thickens, and the crow
    Makes wing to the rooky wood;
    Good things of day begin to droop and drowse,
    Whiles night's black agents to their preys do rouse.
    Thou marvell'st at my words: but hold thee still;
55 Things bad begun make strong themselves by ill:
    So, prithee, go with me.   [*Exeunt*

Scene 3   *A park, with a road leading to the palace*

       Enter three Murderers
     First Murderer
But who did bid thee join with us?
     Third Murderer   Macbeth.
     Second Murderer
He needs not our mistrust, since he delivers
Our offices and what we have to do
To the direction just.
     First Murderer   Then stand with us.
5 The west yet glimmers with some streaks of day:
    Now spurs the lated traveller apace
    To gain the timely inn; and near approaches
    The subject of our watch.
     Third Murderer   Hark! I hear horses.
     Banquo
[*Offstage*] Give us a light there, ho!
     Second Murderer   Then 'tis he: the rest
10 That are within the note of expectation
    Already are i' the court.
     First Murderer   His horses go about.
     Third Murderer
Almost a mile; but he does usually,
So all men do, from hence to the palace gate
Make it their walk.
     Second Murderer
A light, a light!
     Third Murderer   'Tis he.
     First Murderer
15 Stand to 't.

       Enter Banquo *and* Fleance, *with a torch*

Banquo

It will be rain to-night.

      First Murderer   Let it come down.

                    [*They attack* Banquo

      Banquo

O, treachery! Fly, good Fleance, fly, fly, fly!

Thou mayst revenge. O slave!

                 [*Dies.* Fleance *escapes*

      Third Murderer

Who did strike out the light?

      First Murderer   Was 't not the way?

      Third Murderer

20 There's but one down; the son is fled.

      Second Murderer   We have lost

Best half of our affair.

      First Murderer

Well, let's away, and say how much is done.

                      [*Exeunt*

Act 3   scene 4

Macbeth and his wife welcome the guests to their state banquet. The Ghost of Banquo appears, but only Macbeth can see it. Lady Macbeth and the other guests are startled by Macbeth's strange behaviour.

1 *degrees :* social ranks (which would determine the order in which the guests should sit).

3 *society :* the company.

5 *keeps her state :* remains seated on the throne of state.
   in best time : at the right moment.

6 *require her welcome :* request her to welcome you.

Scene 4 *The banqueting hall in the palace*

     Enter Macbeth, Lady Macbeth, Ross,
     Lennox, Lords, *and* Attendants.

      Macbeth

You know your own degrees; sit down: at first and
   last,

The hearty welcome.

      Lords   Thanks to your majesty.

      Macbeth

Ourself will mingle with society

And play the humble host.

5 Our hostess keeps her state, but in best time

We will require her welcome.

      Lady Macbeth

Pronounce it for me, sir, to all our friends;

For my heart speaks they are welcome.

Enter first Murderer

Macbeth
See, they encounter thee with their hearts' thanks;
10 Both sides are even: here I'll sit i' the midst:
Be large in mirth; anon, we'll drink a measure
The table round. [*He goes to the door*] There's blood
    upon thy face.
Murderer
'Tis Banquo's, then.
Macbeth
'Tis better thee without than he within.
15 Is he dispatch'd?
Murderer
My lord, his throat is cut; that I did for him.
Macbeth
Thou art the best o' the cut-throats; yet he's good
That did the like for Fleance: if thou didst it,
Thou art the nonpareil.
Murderer   Most royal sir,
20 Fleance is 'scap'd.
Macbeth
Then comes my fit again: I had else been perfect;
Whole as the marble, founded as the rock,
As broad and general as the casing air:
But now I am cabin'd, cribb'd, confin'd, bound in
25 To saucy doubts and fears. But Banquo's safe?
Murderer
Ay, my good lord; safe in a ditch he bides,
With twenty trenched gashes on his head,
The least a death to nature.
Macbeth   Thanks for that.
There the grown serpent lies: the worm that's fled
30 Hath nature that in time will venom breed,
No teeth for the present. Get thee gone; to-morrow
We'll hear ourselves again.   [*Exit* Murderer
Lady Macbeth   My royal lord,
You do not give the cheer: the feast is sold
That is not often vouch'd, while 'tis a-making,
35 'Tis given with welcome: to feed were best at home;

---

9   *encounter*: greet.
10   *Both sides are even*: there are equal numbers of people sitting on each side of the table.
11   *Be large in mirth*: enjoy yourselves fully.
     anon: presently.
     measure. A cup of wine would be passed round the table, and each man would drink from it.
15   *dispatch'd*: dealt with (i.e. killed).
18   *the like*: the same.
19   *the nonpareil*: the best, without an equal.
21   *fit*: spasm of fear.
     else: otherwise.
     perfect: completely safe.
22-3 Solid as marble, firm as a rock, as free and unconfined as the air surrounding us.
24   *cabin'd, cribb'd*: shut up as if in a small cabin or hut.
25   *saucy*: intruding.
27   *trenched*: hacked.
28   The smallest of the wounds would cause a man's death.
30-1 It will by nature grow into a poisonous snake, but is not dangerous at present.
32   *hear ourselves*: talk together.
33   *give the cheer*: entertain people (as a host should do).
33-5 *the feast . . . welcome*. A banquet is no better than a meal that is sold unless, during the course of the banquet ('while 'tis a-making'), the guests are often told by the host how welcome they are.
35-7 Eating is best at home, but away from home the courtesies of a formal occasion give the food an extra sauce; without this 'sauce' of ceremony, a gathering of people for a meal would be poor. Lady Macbeth makes a pun on 'meat' and 'meet'.

From thence, the sauce to meat is ceremony;
Meeting were bare without it.

Macbeth   Sweet remembrancer!
Now good digestion wait on appetite,
And health on both!

Lennox   May it please your highness sit?

The Ghost *of* Banquo *enters, and sits in*
Macbeth's *place*

Macbeth
40 Here had we now our country's honour roof'd,
Were the grac'd person of our Banquo present;
Who may I rather challenge for unkindness
Than pity for mischance!

Ross   His absence, sir,
Lays blame upon his promise. Please 't your highness
45 To grace us with your royal company?

Macbeth
The table 's full.

Lennox   Here is a place reserv'd, sir.

Macbeth
Where?

Lennox
Here, my good lord. What is 't that moves your
highness?

Macbeth
Which of you have done this?

Lords   What, my good lord?

Macbeth
50 Thou canst not say I did it: never shake
Thy gory locks at me.

Ross
Gentlemen, rise; his highness is not well.

Lady Macbeth
Sit, worthy friends: my lord is often thus,
And hath been from his youth: pray you, keep seat;
55 The fit is momentary; upon a thought
He will again be well. If much you note him,

37   *remembrancer :* reminder (this may mean either Lady Macbeth, or the words she has spoken).

40   *country's honour :* the nobility of the land.
   roof'd : complete (as a house is completed when the roof is put on).

42   *challenge for unkindness :* rebuke for lack of courtesy.

43-4 *His . . . promise :* by not being present, he is at fault for promising to come.

44   *Please 't :* may it please.

47   *Where?* Only Macbeth can see the Ghost.

55   *upon a thought :* as fast as you can think it.

56   *note :* take notice of.

You shall offend him and extend his passion:
Feed, and regard him not. [*Aside to* Macbeth] Are
    you a man?
    Macbeth
Ay, and a bold one, that dare look on that
60 Which might appal the devil.
    Lady Macbeth   O proper stuff!
This is the very painting of your fear;
This is the air-drawn dagger which, you said,
Led you to Duncan. O these flaws and starts—
Impostors to true fear—would well become
65 A woman's story at a winter's fire,
Authoriz'd by her grandam. Shame itself!
Why do you make such faces? When all's done,
You look but on a stool.
    Macbeth
Prithee, see there! behold! look! lo! how say you?
70 Why, what care I? If thou canst nod, speak too.
If charnel-houses and our graves must send
Those that we bury back, our monuments
Shall be the maws of kites.   [*Ghost* disappears
    Lady Macbeth What! quite unmann'd in folly?
    Macbeth
If I stand here, I saw him.
    Lady Macbeth   Fie, for shame!
    Macbeth
75 Blood hath been shed ere now, i' the olden time,
Ere human statute purg'd the gentle weal;
Ay, and since too, murders have been perform'd
Too terrible for the ear: the times have been,
That, when the brains were out, the man would die,
80 And there an end; but now they rise again,
With twenty mortal murders on their crowns,
And push us from our stools: this is more strange
Than such a murder is.
    Lady Macbeth   My worthy lord,
Your noble friends do lack you.
    Macbeth   I do forget.

---

60   *O proper stuff :* Oh rubbish!
61   *This . . . fear :* this is indeed only
      pictured for you by your fear.
62   *air-drawn :* drawn in the air.
63   *flaws and starts :* outbursts and
      alarms.

66   *grandam :* grandmother.

71–3   If tombs ('charnel-houses') and
       graves allow the dead to return to life,
       we shall be forced to use as tombs
       ('monuments') the stomachs ('maws')
       of birds of prey ('kites').
73   *quite . . . folly :* has your foolishness
       made you completely forget that you
       are a man?

75–80 Once upon a time, before man's
       laws made the country ('weal') civilized
       ('gentle'), there was bloodshed; and
       since then, too, there have been
       dreadful murders. But in those days,
       when his brains had been knocked out,
       a man would die, and that was the end
       of it.
81   *mortal murders :* fatal wounds.
       crowns : heads.

85	*muse :* wonder.

85 Do not muse at me, my most worthy friends;
I have a strange infirmity, which is nothing
To those that know me. Come, love and health
   to all;
Then, I'll sit down. Give me some wine; fill full.
I drink to the general joy of the whole table,

91-2   To all of you, and to Banquo,
I will drink a toast, and we will all
drink to each other.

90 And to our dear friend Banquo, whom we miss;
Would he were here! to all, and him, we thirst,
And all to all.

92   *the pledge :* the oath of allegiance
to the king.

      Lords   Our duties, and the pledge.

    Enter Ghost
    Macbeth

93   *Avaunt :* Away!

Avaunt! and quit my sight! Let the earth hide thee!
Thy bones are marrowless, thy blood is cold;

95   *speculation :* intelligent sight.

95 Thou hast no speculation in those eyes
Which thou dost glare with.

    Lady Macbeth   Think of this, good peers,

97   *thing of custom :* regular
occurrence.

But as a thing of custom: 'tis no other;
Only it spoils the pleasure of the time.

    Macbeth
What man dare, I dare:

101   *arm'd :* i.e. with thick skin and
a tusk, like armour and a sword.
    Hyrcan tiger. Tigers of Hircania
(in Persia) were very fierce.
104   *dare :* challenge.
105   *If . . . then :* if I live in fear and
trembling then.
    protest : proclaim.
106   *baby of a girl :* baby girl.

100 Approach thou like the rugged Russian bear,
The arm'd rhinoceros, or the Hyrcan tiger;
Take any shape but that, and my firm nerves
Shall never tremble: or be alive again,
And dare me to the desert with thy sword;
105 If trembling I inhabit then, protest me
The baby of a girl. Hence, horrible shadow!
Unreal mockery, hence!   [Ghost *vanishes*
                    Why, so; being gone,
I am a man again. Pray you, sit still.

    Lady Macbeth

109   *displac'd :* upset.

You have displac'd the mirth, broke the good
   meeting,
110 With most admir'd disorder.

    Macbeth   Can such things be

112-13   *You . . . owe :* you make me feel
like a stranger to my own nature.

And overcome us like a summer's cloud,
Without our special wonder? You make me strange
Even to the disposition that I owe,

116   *mine :* the redness of his cheeks.
       blanch'd : turned white.

119   Pay no attention to the formalities
       with which you should leave.

122   *blood . . . blood :* murder demands
       to be avenged with the death of the
       murderer.
123   *Stones . . . move :* i.e. to reveal a
       buried corpse.
124-6 Speaking birds (such as the
       magpie, jackdaw, and rook) have
       given omens and signs ('Augurs') that
       can be understood, to reveal the most
       secretive murderer.
126   *What is the night :* what time (of
       night) is it?
127   *at odds :* disputing with.
       which is which : whether it is night
       or morning.
128   *denies his person :* refuses to come
       himself.

131-2 I have a paid servant (a spy) in
       every man's house.
132   *will :* will go.
133   *betimes :* early.
134   *bent :* determined.
135   *By the worst means :* in the worst
       way.
135-6 Everything shall be sacrificed
       (made to 'give way') to what I want.
138   *tedious :* troublesome.
       as go o'er : as to cross to the other
       side.
139   *will to hand :* need to be done.
140   They must be performed before
       they are studied.

When now I think you can behold such sights,
115 And keep the natural ruby of your cheeks,
When mine is blanch'd with fear.
          Ross   What sights, my lord?
          Lady Macbeth
I pray you, speak not; he grows worse and worse;
Question enrages him. At once, good-night:
Stand not upon the order of your going,
120 But go at once.
          Lennox   Good-night; and better health
Attend his majesty!
          Lady Macbeth   A kind good-night to all!
                    [*Exeunt* Lords *and* Attendants
          Macbeth
It will have blood, they say; blood will have blood:
Stones have been known to move and trees to
     speak;
Augurs and understood relations have
125 By maggot-pies, and choughs, and rooks, brought
     forth
The secret'st man of blood. What is the night?
          Lady Macbeth
Almost at odds with morning, which is which.
          Macbeth
How sayst thou, that Macduff denies his person
At our great bidding?
          Lady Macbeth   Did you send to him, sir?
          Macbeth
130 I hear it by the way; but I will send.
There's not a one of them but in his house
I keep a servant fee'd. I will to-morrow—
And betimes I will—to the weird sisters:
More shall they speak; for now I am bent to know,
135 By the worst means, the worst. For mine own good
All causes shall give way: I am in blood
Stepp'd in so far, that, should I wade no more,
Returning were as tedious as go o'er.
Strange things I have in head that will to hand,
140 Which must be acted ere they may be scann'd.

141   *season*: preservative.

142-3   My strange self-deception is like the fear of a beginner ('initiate') who needs practice.
144   *young*: inexperienced.

Act 3   scene 5
The Witches meet again, and Hecate, their Queen, scolds them for speaking to Macbeth. She orders them to meet her at another time, when Macbeth will come to ask for more knowledge. This scene was probably not written by Shakespeare, but added to the play because the audience liked to see the witches.

2   *beldams*: old hags.
3   *Saucy*: impudent.
4   *traffic*: deal.

7   *close contriver*: secret planner.

9   *art*: i.e. witchcraft.

12-13   Macbeth does not love evil for its own sake, but only for what it can do for him.

15   *Acheron*: a river in the Greek underworld.

24   *vaporous drop profound*. It was believed that the moon shed a foam, with magical powers ('profound'), on to various herbs.
26   *sleights*: tricks.
27   *sprites*: spirits, ghosts.
29   *confusion*: damnation.

Lady Macbeth
You lack the season of all natures, sleep.
Macbeth
Come, we'll to sleep. My strange and self-abuse
Is the initiate fear that wants hard use:
We are yet but young in deed.   [*Exeunt*

Scene 5 *On the moor*

Thunder. Enter the three Witches, *meeting* Hecate
First Witch
Why, how now, Hecate! you look angrily.
Hecate
Have I not reason, beldams as you are,
Saucy and overbold? How did you dare
To trade and traffic with Macbeth
5 In riddles and affairs of death;
And I, the mistress of your charms,
The close contriver of all harms,
Was never call'd to bear my part,
Or show the glory of our art?
10 And, which is worse, all you have done
Hath been but for a wayward son,
Spiteful and wrathful; who, as others do,
Loves for his own ends, not for you.
But make amends now: get you gone,
15 And at the pit of Acheron
Meet me i' the morning: thither he
Will come to know his destiny:
Your vessels and your spells provide,
Your charms and everything beside.
20 I am for the air; this night I'll spend
Unto a dismal and a fatal end:
Great business must be wrought ere noon:
Upon the corner of the moon
There hangs a vaporous drop profound;
25 I'll catch it ere it come to ground:
And that, distill'd by magic sleights,
Shall raise such artificial sprites
As by the strength of their illusion
Shall draw him on to his confusion:

30-1   He will have high hopes, above the reach of wisdom.

32   *security :* over-confidence.

30   He shall spurn fate, scorn death, and bear
His hopes 'bove wisdom, grace, and fear;
And you all know, security
Is mortals' chiefest enemy.
    [*A song is sung offstage*
Hark! I am call'd; my little spirit, see,
35   Sits in a foggy cloud, and stays for me.   [*Exit*
    First Witch
Come, let's make haste; she'll soon be back again.
    [*Exeunt*

Act 3   scene 6

Lennox talks to another Lord, and reminds him of what has happened. We can tell from the irony of his words that Lennox (and probably many others) is now suspicious of Macbeth. The Lord can give some information about Duncan's son Malcolm, and about Macduff.

1-2   I have only spoken what you are thinking, and your own thoughts can work out the meaning in full.
3   *borne :* managed.
4   *marry :* by [the Virgin] Mary; the oath was very commonly used, and is not strong.
8   *cannot . . . thought :* can fail to think.
10   *fact :* deed.
11   *straight :* immediately.

13   *thralls :* captives.

16   *deny 't :* deny that they had murdered Duncan.
17   *borne :* managed.
18   *under his key :* locked up.
19   *an't :* if.

21   *broad words :* gossip.

24   *bestows himself :* is staying.

Scene 6 *Forres. A room in the palace*

Enter Lennox *and another* Lord

    Lennox
My former speeches have but hit your thoughts,
Which can interpret further: only, I say,
Things have been strangely borne. The gracious Duncan
Was pitied of Macbeth: marry, he was dead:
5   And the right-valiant Banquo walk'd too late;
Whom, you may say, if 't please you, Fleance kill'd,
For Fleance fled: men must not walk too late.
Who cannot want the thought, how monstrous
It was for Malcolm and for Donalbain
10   To kill their gracious father? damned fact!
How it did grieve Macbeth! did he not straight
In pious rage the two delinquents tear,
That were the slaves of drink and thralls of sleep?
Was not that nobly done? Ay, and wisely too;
15   For 'twould have anger'd any heart alive
To hear the men deny 't. So that, I say,
He has borne all things well; and I do think
That, had he Duncan's sons under his key—
As, an't please heaven, he shall not—they should find
20   What 'twere to kill a father; so should Fleance.
But, peace! for from broad words, and 'cause he fail'd
His presence at the tyrant's feast, I hear
Macduff lives in disgrace. Sir, can you tell
Where he bestows himself?

25   *holds . . . birth*: witholds his birth-
right (i.e. the crown).

27   *Of*: by.
Edward: Edward the Confessor,
king of England 1042–66.

28-9   He does not lose any honour
because of his misfortunes.

30   *upon his aid*: in support of Malcolm.

31   Siward, Earl of Northumberland,
and Young Siward, his son.

33   *ratify*: sanction.

36   *free*: honest.

38   *exasperate*: angered.

40   *absolute*: curt.
'*Sir, not I*'. This was Macduff's
reply to Macbeth.

41   *cloudy*: sullen.
turns me. The word 'me' here is
used for emphasis only.

42   *hums*: murmurs.

43   *clogs*: burdens. The messenger
would know that Macbeth was angry
with messengers who brought bad
news—see 5, 5, 38-40.

44   Warn him to be cautious and keep
as far from Macbeth as his wisdom can
take him.

Lord   The son of Duncan,
25   From whom this tyrant holds the due of birth,
Lives in the English court, and is receiv'd
Of the most pious Edward with such grace
That the malevolence of fortune nothing
Takes from his high respect. Thither Macduff
30   Is gone to pray the holy king, upon his aid
To wake Northumberland and war-like Siward:
That, by the help of these—with Him above
To ratify the work—we may again
Give to our tables meat, sleep to our nights,
35   Free from our feasts and banquets bloody knives,
Do faithful homage and receive free honours;
All which we pine for now. And this report
Hath so exasperate the king that he
Prepares for some attempt of war.
Lennox   Sent he to Macduff?
Lord
40   He did: and with an absolute, 'Sir, not I,'
The cloudy messenger turns me his back,
And hums, as who should say, 'You'll rue the time
That clogs me with this answer.'
Lennox   And that well might
Advise him to a caution to hold what distance
45   His wisdom can provide. Some holy angel
Fly to the court of England and unfold
His message ere he come, that a swift blessing
May soon return to this our suffering country
Under a hand accurs'd!
Lord   I'll send my prayers with him!
                                              [*Exeunt*

Act 4

Act 4   scene 1

The witches gather on the moor to meet Macbeth. He makes them promise to answer his questions, and they conjure up magic apparitions which at first comfort, and then alarm him.

1   *brinded* : brindled (brown, with stripes of some other colour).

2   *hedge-pig* : hedgehog (a small wild animal with a snout like a pig's, covered with sharp prickles).

3   *Harpier* : the name of the witch's 'familiar' (see *Macbeth:* **The play p. ix.**) perhaps suggested to Shakespeare by the word 'harpy'—a monster, half-woman and half-bird, in Greek mythology.

8   *swelter'd* : sweated.
     venom : poison. All the ingredients of the witches' cooking-pot were thought by the Elizabethans to be poisonous, or at least unnatural.
     sleeping got : caught while it was asleep.

12   *Fillet* : slice.
     fenny : from the fens (low-lying, marshy land).

15   *Wool of bat* : the short hair nearest the skin of a bat (which is a smooth-haired animal).

16   *fork* : forked tongue.
     blind-worm : slow-worm (a kind of legless lizard).

17   *howlet* : owlet (a baby owl).

19   *hell-broth* : a thick soup, strong enough for the devil.

23   *mummy* : a medicine, either powder or liquid, made by witches and also by reputable doctors, from dead bodies.
     maw and gulf : stomach and throat.

Scene 1 *A cave on the moor. In the centre is a boiling cauldron*

Thunder. Enter the three Witches
First Witch
Thrice the brinded cat hath mew'd.
Second Witch
Thrice and once the hedge-pig whin'd.
Third Witch
Harpier cries: 'Tis time, 'tis time.
First Witch
Round about the cauldron go;   5
In the poison'd entrails throw.
Toad, that under cold stone
Days and nights hast thirty-one
Swelter'd venom, sleeping got,
Boil thou first i' the charmed pot.   10
    All
Double, double, toil and trouble;
Fire burn and cauldron bubble.
Second Witch
Fillet of a fenny snake,
In the cauldron boil and bake;
Eye of newt, and toe of frog,   15
Wool of bat, and tongue of dog,
Adder's fork, and blind-worm's sting,
Lizard's leg, and howlet's wing,
For a charm of powerful trouble,
Like a hell-broth boil and bubble.   20
    All
Double, double, toil and trouble;
Fire burn and cauldron bubble.
Third Witch
Scale of dragon, tooth of wolf,
Witches' mummy, maw and gulf

24   *ravin'd :* glutted (so its stomach would be full of human flesh).

25   *i' the dark.* Night was the best time for gathering poisonous herbs and roots.

27   *slips :* cuttings.

28   *Sliver'd :* sliced off.

31   *Ditch-deliver'd :* born in a ditch.
     drab : whore.

32   *slab :* sticky.

33   *chaudron :* entrails.

39-43   These lines, like the whole of *Act 3*, scene 5, were probably not written by Shakespeare.

39   I am pleased by the trouble that you have taken.

50   I call upon you, in the name of the magic that you practice.

51   *Howe'er . . . it :* i.e. even if you have learned it from the devil.

53   *yesty :* yeasty (because they foam, like a liquid to which yeast has been added).

Of the ravin'd salt-sea shark,
25   Root of hemlock digg'd i' the dark,
Liver of blaspheming Jew,
Gall of goat, and slips of yew
Sliver'd in the moon's eclipse,
Nose of Turk, and Tartar's lips,
30   Finger of birth-strangled babe
Ditch-deliver'd by a drab,
Make the gruel thick and slab;
Add thereto a tiger's chaudron,
For the ingredients of our cauldron.

All
35   Double, double, toil and trouble;
Fire burn and cauldron bubble.

Second Witch
Cool it with a baboon's blood,
Then the charm is firm and good.

Enter Hecate
Hecate
O well done! I commend your pains,
40   And every one shall share i' the gains.
And now about the cauldron sing,
Like elves and fairies in a ring,
Enchanting all that you put in.

                                        [*They sing*

Second Witch
By the pricking of my thumbs,
45   Something wicked this way comes.
Open, locks,
Whoever knocks.

Enter Macbeth
Macbeth
How now, you secret, black, and midnight hags!
What is 't you do?
All   A deed without a name.
Macbeth
50   I conjure you, by that which you profess—
Howe'er you come to know it—answer me:
Though you untie the winds and let them fight
Against the churches; though the yesty waves

54   *Confound* : confuse.
      navigation : shipping.
55   *bladed* : unripe (the corn is still a
      'blade', not yet an 'ear').
      lodg'd : blown flat.
57   *slope* : bend.

59   *Nature's germens* : the seeds of all
      creation.
60   *till destruction sicken* : until
      destruction itself is sick (because so
      much has been destroyed).

63   *our masters* : i.e. the evil spirits they
      serve.

65   *nine farrow* : litter of nine piglets
      (only an unnatural sow would do this,
      and therefore her blood would be
      poisonous).
      sweaten : sweated.
68   *office* : function.
68sd *Apparition.* The Apparitions rose
      through a trapdoor in the stage, and
      then 'descended' again.

73   *caution* : advice.
74   *harp'd* : guessed.
      aright : correctly.

Confound and swallow navigation up;
55 Though bladed corn be lodg'd, and trees blown
      down;
   Though castles topple on their warders' heads;
   Though palaces and pyramids do slope
   Their heads to their foundations; though the
      treasure
   Of Nature's germens tumble all together,
60 Even till destruction sicken—answer me
   To what I ask you.
      First Witch   Speak.
      Second Witch   Demand.
      Third Witch   We'll answer.
      First Witch
   Say if thou'dst rather hear it from our mouths,
   Or from our masters'?
      Macbeth   Call 'em: let me see 'em.
      First Witch
   Pour in sow's blood, that hath eaten
65   Her nine farrow; grease that's sweaten
   From the murderer's gibbet, throw
   Into the flame.
      All   Come, high or low;
   Thyself and office deftly show.

      Thunder. First Apparition *: an armed Head*
      Macbeth
   Tell me, thou unknown power,—
      First Witch   He knows thy thought:
70 Hear his speech, but say thou nought.
      First Apparition
   Macbeth! Macbeth! Macbeth! beware Macduff;
   Beware the Thane of Fife. Dismiss me. Enough.
                                    [*Descends*
      Macbeth
   Whate'er thou art, for thy good caution thanks;
   Thou hast harp'd my fear aright. But one word
      more—
      First Witch
75 He will not be commanded: here's another,

More potent than the first.

> *Thunder. Second* Apparition : *a bloody Child*

Second Apparition

Macbeth! Macbeth! Macbeth!—

Macbeth

Had I three ears, I'd hear thee.

Second Apparition

Be bloody, bold, and resolute; laugh to scorn
80 The power of man, for none of woman born
Shall harm Macbeth.   [*Descends*

Macbeth

Then live, Macduff: what need I fear of thee?
But yet I'll make assurance double sure,
And take a bond of fate: thou shalt not live;
85 That I may tell pale-hearted fear it lies,
And sleep in spite of thunder.

> *Thunder. Third* Apparition : *a Child crowned, with a tree in his hand*

                                      What is this,
That rises like the issue of a king,
And wears upon his baby brow the round
And top of sovereignty?

All   Listen, but speak not to 't.

Third Apparition

90 Be lion-mettl'd, proud, and take no care
Who chafes, who frets, or where conspirers are:
Macbeth shall never vanquish'd be until
Great Birnam Wood to high Dunsinane Hill
Shall come against him.   [*Descends*

Macbeth   That will never be:
95 Who can impress the forest, bid the tree
Unfix his earth-bound root? Sweet bodements!
  good!
Rebellious dead, rise never till the wood
Of Birnam rise, and our high-plac'd Macbeth
Shall live the lease of nature, pay his breath
100 To time and mortal custom. Yet my heart
Throbs to know one thing: tell me—if your art
Can tell so much—shall Banquo's issue ever
Reign in this kingdom?

83-4   I will make doubly sure, and guarantee ('take a bond') that fate keeps its word.

84   *thou* : i.e. Macduff.

85   So that I may tell my fears that they are false.

86   *thunder*. Thunder was often thought to be the voice of God, reminding the evil-doer of his crimes, and warning him to repent.

87   *issue* : offspring.

88-9   *round And top* : i.e. the crown.

90   *lion-mettl'd* : lion-hearted.

91   *chafes* : is angry.
        frets : complains.

93   Birnam Wood was about twelve miles from Dunsinane.

95   *impress* : enlist (as a soldier).

96   *bodements* : prophecies.

99   *the lease of nature* : have a natural lease (or length) of life.

99-100 Give up his breath (as if he were paying a debt) to old age and the natural causes of death.

101   *Throbs* : desires.

111sd   *show* : dumb-show.
    glass. This might be either a
mirror, held in such a way that it
reflected several more kings behind the
eighth, or else some kind of magic
'crystal ball'.

112–24   The eight kings pass, one at
    a time, in front of Macbeth, and he
    comments on each one as it passes
    him.

113   *sear* : burn.
    hair : appearance.

116   *Start, eyes* : let my eyeballs fall
    from their sockets.

117   *crack of doom* : the dawning of
    Doomsday.

121   The double orb refers to the
    coronation of King James at both
    Scone (as James VI of Scotland) and
    Westminster (as James I of England);
    a single sceptre is used in the Scottish
    ceremony, and two in the English
    coronation. See Introduction, p. v.
    See illustration, p. 65.

123   *blood-bolter'd* : hair clotted with
    blood.

All   Seek to know no more.
    Macbeth
    I will be satisfied: deny me this,
105 And an eternal curse fall on you! Let me know.
    Why sinks that cauldron? and what noise is this?
                            [*Music; the cauldron descends*

    First Witch
    Show!
    Second Witch
    Show!
    Third Witch
    Show!
    All
110 Show his eyes, and grieve his heart;
    Come like shadows, so depart.

            *A show of Eight Kings; the last with a glass
            in his hand :* Banquo *following*

    Macbeth
    Thou art too like the spirit of Banquo; down!
    Thy crown does sear mine eyeballs: and thy hair,
    Thou other gold-bound brow, is like the first:
115 A third is like the former. Filthy hags!
    Why do you show me this? A fourth! Start, eyes!
    What! will the line stretch out to the crack of doom?
    Another yet? A seventh! I'll see no more:
    And yet the eighth appears, who bears a glass
120 Which shows me many more; and some I see
    That two-fold balls and treble sceptres carry.
    Horrible sight! Now, I see, 'tis true;
    For the blood-bolter'd Banquo smiles upon me,
    And points at them for his.   [*Apparitions vanish*
                            What! is this so?
    First Witch
125 Ay, sir, all this is so: but why
    Stands Macbeth thus amazedly?
    Come sisters, cheer we up his sprites,
    And show the best of our delights.
    I'll charm the air to give a sound,
130 While you perform your antick round,
    That this great king may kindly say
    Our duties did his welcome pay.

127   *sprites*: spirits.
130   *antick round*: comic dance (in a circle around Macbeth).
132   Our homage has paid him the welcome due to him.
134   *aye*: for ever.
135   *without there*: whoever is outside (offstage).

145-6   You can never be as fast as you intend to be unless you perform a deed as soon as you think of it.
147-8   The first conceptions of my heart shall be the first acts of my hand.
149   *crown*: complete.

151   *Fife*: i.e. Macduff.

153   *trace . . . line*: descend from him, are of his lineage.

155   *sights*: the apparitions.

[*Music. The Witches dance, and then vanish with* Hecate

Macbeth
Where are they? Gone? Let this pernicious hour
Stand aye accursed in the calendar!

135   Come in, without there!

Enter Lennox

Lennox   What's your Grace's will?

Macbeth
Saw you the weird sisters?

Lennox   No, my lord.

Macbeth
Came they not by you?

Lennox   No indeed, my lord.

Macbeth
Infected be the air whereon they ride,
And damn'd all those that trust them! I did hear

140   The galloping of horse: who was 't came by?

Lennox
'Tis two or three, my lord, that bring you word
Macduff is fled to England.

Macbeth   Fled to England!

Lennox
Ay, my good lord.

Macbeth
[*Aside*] Time, thou anticipat'st my dread exploits;

145   The flighty purpose never is o'ertook
Unless the deed go with it; from this moment
The very firstlings of my heart shall be
The firstlings of my hand. And even now,
To crown my thoughts with acts, be it thought and done:

150   The castle of Macduff I will surprise;
Seize upon Fife; give to the edge of the sword
His wife, his babes, and all unfortunate souls
That trace him in his line. No boasting like a fool;
This deed I'll do before this purpose cool:

155   But no more sights! [*Aloud*] Where are these gentlemen?
Come, bring me where they are.   [*Exeunt*

Act 4   scene 2

Lady Macduff questions Ross about
her husband's flight, and then tries to
explain the situation to her little son.
A Messenger warns her to flee from
the palace, but it is too late. The
murderers rush into the room.

3-4   When we are not traitors for
what we have done, we are still traitors
by being afraid and running away.

7   *titles*: possessions, things he is
entitled to.

9   *wants*: lacks.
natural touch: instincts.

12-15   When it is so unreasonable to run
away, it shows neither love (for his
family) nor wisdom, but only fear (for
himself).

14   *coz*: cousin (but they are probably
not related).

15   *school*: control.
for: as for.

16   *judicious*: of good judgement.

17   *fits o' the season*: moods of the
times.

18-19   *we are . . . ourselves*: we are false
to those things we say we believe in,
and we do not understand our own
actions.

19-20   Fears make us believe rumours.

22   *Each . . . move*: move backwards
and forwards.

23   *Shall*: it will.
but: before.

24   *climb upward*: improve.

Scene 2 *Fife. A room in Macduff's castle*

Enter Lady Macduff, *her* Son, *and* Ross

Lady Macduff
What had he done to make him fly the land?

Ross
You must have patience, madam.

Lady Macduff   He had none:
His flight was madness: when our actions do not,
Our fears do make us traitors.

Ross   You know not
5 Whether it was his wisdom or his fear.

Lady Macduff
Wisdom! to leave his wife, to leave his babes,
His mansion and his titles in a place
From whence himself does fly? He loves us not;
He wants the natural touch; for the poor wren,
10 The most diminutive of birds, will fight—
Her young ones in her nest—against the owl.
All is the fear and nothing is the love;
As little is the wisdom, where the flight
So runs against all reason.

Ross   My dearest coz,
15 I pray you, school yourself: but, for your husband,
He is noble, wise, judicious, and best knows
The fits o' the season. I dare not speak much further:
But cruel are the times, when we are traitors
And do not know ourselves; when we hold rumour
20 From what we fear, yet know not what we fear,
But float upon a wild and violent sea
Each way, and move. I take my leave of you:
Shall not be long but I'll be here again.
Things at the worst will cease, or else climb upward
25 To what they were before. My pretty cousin,
Blessing upon you!

28-9 If Ross were to stay, he would be
so foolish as to weep; this would be
a disgrace to him, and an embarrass-
ment to Lady Macduff.

30 *Sirrah.* A term of endearment (as
used here), or abuse.

34 *lime.* The birds' feet stuck in the
lime, and they were caught.

35 *pit-fall* : snare.
gin : trap.

36 *Poor . . . for* : they are not set to
catch poor birds (only those with rich
plumage).

41 If you can get them so easily, you
will not want to keep them.

42 *wit* : intelligence.

43 *for thee* : for your age.

Lady Macduff
Father'd he is, and yet he's fatherless.

Ross
I am so much a fool, should I stay longer,
It would be my disgrace, and your discomfort:
30 I take my leave at once.   [*Exit*

Lady Macduff   Sirrah, your father's dead:
And what will you do now? How will you live?

Son
As birds do, mother.

Lady Macduff   What! with worms and flies?

Son
With what I get, I mean; and so do they.

Lady Macduff
Poor bird! thou'dst never fear the net nor lime,
35 The pit-fall nor the gin?

Son
Why should I, mother? Poor birds they are not
     set for.
My father is not dead, for all your saying.

Lady Macduff
Yes, he is dead: how wilt thou do for a father?

Son
Nay, how will you do for a husband?

Lady Macduff
40 Why, I can buy me twenty at any market.

Son
Then you'll buy 'em to sell again.

Lady Macduff
Thou speak'st with all thy wit; and yet, i' faith,
With wit enough for thee.

Son
Was my father a traitor, mother?

Lady Macduff
45 Ay, that he was.

Son
What is a traitor?

Lady Macduff
Why, one that swears and lies.

Son
And be all traitors that do so?

Lady Macduff
Every one that does so is a traitor, and must be
hanged.

Son
50 And must they all be hanged that swear and lie?

Lady Macduff
Every one.

Son
Who must hang them?

Lady Macduff
Why, the honest men.

Son
Then the liars and swearers are fools, for there are
55 liars and swearers enow to beat the honest men,
and hang up them.

Lady Macduff
Now God help thee, poor monkey! But how wilt
thou do for a father?

Son
If he were dead, you'd weep for him: if you would
60 not, it were a good sign that I should quickly have
a new father.

Lady Macduff
Poor prattler, how thou talk'st!

Enter a Messenger

Messenger
Bless you, fair dame! I am not to you known,
Though in your state of honour I am perfect.
65 I doubt some danger does approach you nearly:
If you will take a homely man's advice,
Be not found here; hence, with your little ones.
To fright you thus, methinks, I am too savage;
To do worse to you were fell cruelty,
70 Which is too nigh your person. Heaven preserve
you!
I dare abide no longer.   [*Exit*

Lady Macduff   Whither should I fly?
I have done no harm. But I remember now,
I am in this earthly world, where to do harm
Is often laudable, to do good sometime

55   *enow :* enough.

59–60   *would not :* would not weep.

62   *prattler :* chatterbox.

64   I know your rank very well.
65   *doubt :* suspect.
       nearly : closely.
66   *homely :* humble.

68   *savage :* cruel.
69   *fell :* pitiless.
70   Which is already too close to you.

75 Accounted dangerous folly; why then, alas!
Do I put up that womanly defence,
To say I have done no harm?

Enter Murderers

What are these faces?

Murderer
Where is your husband?
Lady Macduff
I hope in no place so unsanctified
80 Where such as thou mayst find him.
Murderer   He's a traitor.
Son
Thou liest, thou shag-hair'd villain.
Murderer   What, you egg!
Young fry of treachery!   [*Stabbing him*
Son   He has kill'd me, mother:
Run away, I pray you!   [*Dies*
[*Exit* Lady Macduff, *crying* 'Murder', *and*
pursued by the Murderers

81 *shag-hair'd :* with shaggy hair.

82 *fry :* spawn, young fish.

Act 4   scene 3
Safely away from Scotland, Macduff
has been telling Malcolm about the
sufferings of his country. At first
Malcolm does not trust Macduff. He
tells him that he (Malcolm) will be a
greater tyrant than Macbeth, because
he has more vices. Macduff is
distressed, but when Malcolm sees
the sorrow he explains that he told lies
about himself to test Macduff's
loyalty. We hear about the holy
English king, whose touch cures
sickness. Ross brings bad news to
Macduff.

2   *bosoms :* hearts.
3   *mortal :* deadly.
4   *Bestride :* defend.
      birthdom : country of our birth.
6–8   The grief cries up to heaven, and
      the skies seem to feel Scotland's
      sorrow, for heaven's cries echo the
      same note.
8   *Like :* the same.
8–10 I will lament for what I believe,
      believe only what I know to be true,
      and do what I can to put things right
      when the time is favourable ('to
      friend').

Scene 3 *England. Outside the king's palace*

Enter Malcolm *and* Macduff

Malcolm
Let us seek out some desolate shade, and there
Weep our sad bosoms empty.
Macduff   Let us rather
Hold fast the mortal sword, and like good men
Bestride our down-fall'n birthdom. Each new morn
5 New widows howl, new orphans cry, new sorrows
Strike heaven on the face, that it resounds
As if it felt with Scotland, and yell'd out
Like syllable of dolour.
Malcolm   What I believe I'll wail,
What know, believe; and what I can redress,

11   Perhaps what you say is true.

12   *whose sole name :* whose name alone.

14   *touch'd :* harmed.

14-15 *I am . . . me :* although I am only
young, you may gain something from
him by betraying me.

15   *wisdom :* it is good sense.

16   *lamb :* Malcolm means himself.

19   *recoil :* turn away from virtue.

20   *In . . . charge :* at a royal command.
      crave : beg.

21   My thoughts cannot change your
nature.

22   Although Lucifer, the 'brightest'
angel, fell from God's grace, we must
not assume that all angels are like him;
some are pure and 'bright' still.

23-4   Although evil tries to look
virtuous, virtue is no less virtuous than
it ever was.

5   *Perchance :* perhaps.
      even there. Macduff was hoping
that he could help to overthrow
Macbeth, but in his flight to England
he lost his hopes. But the suddenness
of this flight has aroused Malcolm's
suspicions.

26   *rawness :* exposure to danger.

27   *motives :* incentives.
      knots of love : ties of affection.

28   *leave-taking :* saying 'goodbye'.

29-30 Do not think my suspicions do
you any dishonour; they are to protect
me.

30   *rightly just :* truly honest.

32-4   Tyranny may lay its foundations
securely, since righteousness (in the
person of Malcolm) dare not stop it.
Macbeth can wear his stolen crown,
for his title is confirmed ('affeered'
is a legal term) by Malcolm's weakness.

37   *to boot :* in addition.

38   I do not speak like this just
because I am afraid of you.

39   *yoke :* i.e. the rule of Macbeth.
The 'yoke' fastens oxen to the plough
they are pulling.

41   *withal :* as well.

10 As I shall find the time to friend, I will.
What you have spoke, it may be so, perchance.
This tyrant, whose sole name blisters our tongues,
Was once thought honest; you have lov'd him well;
He hath not touch'd you yet. I am young, but
something
15 You may deserve of him through me, and wisdom
To offer up a weak, poor, innocent lamb
T' appease an angry god.
      Macduff
I am not treacherous.
      Malcolm   But Macbeth is.
A good and virtuous nature may recoil
20 In an imperial charge. But I shall crave your
pardon;
That which you are my thoughts cannot transpose;
Angels are bright still, though the brightest fell;
Though all things foul would wear the brows of
grace,
Yet grace must still look so.
      Macduff   I have lost my hopes.
      Malcolm
25 Perchance even there where I did find my doubts.
Why in that rawness left you wife and child—
Those precious motives, those strong knots of
love—
Without leave-taking? I pray you,
Let not my jealousies be your dishonours,
30 But mine own safeties: you may be rightly just,
Whatever I shall think.
      Macduff   Bleed, bleed, poor country!
Great tyranny, lay thou thy basis sure,
For goodness dare not check thee! wear thou thy
wrongs;
The title is affeer'd! Fare thee well, lord:
35 I would not be the villain that thou think'st
For the whole space that's in the tyrant's grasp,
And the rich East to boot.
      Malcolm   Be not offended:
I speak not as in absolute fear of you.
I think our country sinks beneath the yoke;
40 It weeps, it bleeds, and each new day a gash
Is added to her wounds: I think withal

There would be hands uplifted in my right;
And here from gracious England have I offer
Of goodly thousands. But, for all this,
45 When I shall tread upon the tyrant's head,
Or wear it on my sword, yet my poor country
Shall have more vices than it had before,
More suffer, and more sundry ways than ever,
By him that shall succeed.

Macduff   What should he be?

Malcolm
50 It is myself I mean; in whom I know
All the particulars of vice so grafted,
That, when they shall be open'd, black Macbeth
Will seem as pure as snow, and the poor state
Esteem him as a lamb, being compar'd
55 With my confineless harms.

Macduff   Not in the legions
Of horrid hell can come a devil more damn'd
In evils to top Macbeth.

Malcolm   I grant him bloody,
Luxurious, avaricious, false, deceitful,
Sudden, malicious, smacking of every sin
60 That has a name; but there's no bottom, none,
In my voluptuousness: your wives, your daughters,
Your matrons, and your maids, could not fill up
The cistern of my lust, and my desire
All continent impediments would o'erbear
65 That did oppose my will; better Macbeth
Than such an one to reign.

Macduff   Boundless intemperance
In nature is a tyranny; it hath been
Th' untimely emptying of the happy throne,
And fall of many kings. But fear not yet
70 To take upon you what is yours; you may
Convey your pleasures in a spacious plenty,
And yet seem cold—the time you may so hoodwink.
We have willing dames enough; there cannot be
That vulture in you, to devour so many

43   *gracious England :* i.e. Edward the Confessor.

44   *goodly thousands :* thousands of good soldiers.

46   *wear :* carry.

48-9   Shall suffer more, and suffer in more different ways, than ever before.

51   *particulars of vice :* individual vices.
      grafted : implanted.

52   *open'd :* developed (they have been planted like flowers, and will open as buds open).

55   *confineless harms :* boundless evils.

57   *top :* surpass.

58   *Luxurious :* lustful.

59   *Sudden :* violent.
      smacking : tasting.

61   *voluptuousness :* lechery.

63   *cistern :* tank (as a water-tank).

63-5   My lust would break down all the obstacles that chastity ('continence') set up against my will.

66   *such an one :* a man like this.

66-7   Complete lack of self-control is a tyranny in man's nature.

67-9   It has caused many thrones to become vacant before the proper time.

71   *Convey :* secretly conduct.
      in a spacious plenty : where there is plenty of room.

72   *cold :* chaste.
      the time : the age (or 'the people').
      hoodwink : deceive.

73-6   Who will offer themselves (as mistresses) to the king, as soon as they know what his desires are.

77   *ill-compos'd affection :* unbalanced nature.
78   *staunchless :* unsatisfied.
79   *cut off :* kill.
80   *his . . . house :* this man's jewels, and that man's house.
81   *my more-having :* the more I had.

85   *sticks deeper :* is a more deeply-rooted vice.
86   *summer-seeming lust :* lust is only fit for the summer of man's life, and dies away with the winter of age.
87   *The sword :* the cause of death.
88-9   Scotland has rich harvests ('foisons') of wealth that will satisfy you, merely from your own estates.
89   *portable :* bearable.
90   Balanced against your virtues.
91   *king-becoming graces :* virtues appropriate to a king.
92   *verity :* truth.
       stableness : constancy.
93   *Bounty :* generosity.
       lowliness : humility.
95   *no relish :* no trace.
96   *division :* variations.
       several : separate.
97-8   If I could, I would say 'To hell with harmony'.
99   *Uproar :* cause uproar in.
       confound : destroy.

104   *untitled :* without hereditary right to the throne.
       bloody-scepter'd : Macbeth has obtained the throne through bloodshed, and it is as though his sceptre were stained with blood.
105   *wholesome :* good, healthy.
106   *truest issue :* true heir.
107-8   By banning himself from Scotland, he is convicted ('stands accus'd') of evil, and slanders his family.

75 As will to greatness dedicate themselves,
    Finding it so inclin'd.
    Malcolm   With this there grows
    In my most ill-compos'd affection such
    A staunchless avarice that, were I king,
    I should cut off the nobles for their lands,
80 Desire his jewels and this other's house;
    And my more-having would be as a sauce
    To make me hunger more, that I should forge
    Quarrels unjust against the good and loyal,
    Destroying them for wealth.
    Macduff   This avarice
85 Sticks deeper, grows with more pernicious root
    Than summer-seeming lust; and it hath been
    The sword of our slain kings: yet do not fear;
    Scotland hath foisons to fill up your will,
    Of your mere own; all these are portable
90 With other graces weigh'd.
    Malcolm
    But I have none: the king-becoming graces,
    As justice, verity, temperance, stableness,
    Bounty, perseverance, mercy, lowliness,
    Devotion, patience, courage, fortitude—
95 I have no relish of them, but abound
    In the division of each several crime,
    Acting it many ways. Nay, had I power, I should
    Pour the sweet milk of concord into hell,
    Uproar the universal peace, confound
100 All unity on earth.
    Macduff   O Scotland, Scotland!
    Malcolm
    If such a one be fit to govern, speak;
    I am as I have spoken.
    Macduff   Fit to govern!
    No, not to live. O nation miserable,
    With an untitled tyrant bloody-scepter'd!
105 When shalt thou see thy wholesome days again,
    Since that the truest issue of thy throne
    By his own interdiction stands accus'd,

Edward the Confessor

And does blaspheme his breed? Thy royal father
Was a most sainted king; the queen that bore thee,
Oft'ner upon her knees than on her feet,
Died every day she liv'd. Fare thee well!
These evils thou repeat'st upon thyself
Have banish'd me from Scotland. O my breast,
Thy hope ends here!

Malcolm   Macduff, this noble passion,
Child of integrity, hath from my soul
Wip'd the black scruples, reconcil'd my thoughts
To thy good truth and honour. Devilish Macbeth
By many of these trains hath sought to win me
Into his power, and modest wisdom plucks me
From over-credulous haste; but God above
Deal between thee and me! for even now
I put myself to thy direction, and
Unspeak mine own detraction, here abjure
The taints and blames I laid upon myself,
For strangers to my nature. I am yet
Unknown to woman; never was forsworn;
Scarcely have coveted what was mine own;
At no time broke my faith; would not betray
The devil to his fellow; and delight
No less in truth than life; my first false speaking
Was this upon myself. What I am truly,
Is thine and my poor country's to command;
Whither indeed, before thy here-approach,
Old Siward, with ten thousand warlike men,
Already at a point, was setting forth.
Now we'll together, and the chance of goodness
Be like our warranted quarrel. Why are you silent?

Macduff
Such welcome and unwelcome things at once
'Tis hard to reconcile.

Enter a Doctor

Malcolm   Well, more anon.
Comes the king forth, I pray you?

Doctor
Ay, sir; there are a crew of wretched souls
That stay his cure; their malady convinces

---

110   *upon her knees :* i.e. in prayer.
111   In her prayers, she made a daily vow of rejecting ('dying to') sin.
112   *repeat'st . . . thyself :* accuse yourself of.
113   *breast :* heart.

115   *Child of integrity.* Macduff's grief for Scotland could only spring from honesty.
116   *scruples :* suspicions.
   reconcil'd my thoughts : made me trust you again.
118   *trains :* schemes.
119   *modest :* cautious.
119-20   Prevents me from trusting people too quickly.
120-1   *but . . . me :* but now may God direct the dealings between you and me.
122   *to :* under.
123   I withdraw the accusations I made against myself.
   abjure : renounce.
125   *For strangers :* as foreign.
126   *Unknown to woman :* a virgin.
   was forsworn : committed perjury.

133   *here-approach :* coming here.

135   *at a point :* ready.
136   *we'll together :* we'll go together.
136-7   May our chances of success ('goodness' = good fortune) be the same as the justice (warranty) of the cause ('quarrel') we fight for.

139   *more anon :* we'll talk more about that later (the entry of the Doctor stops their conversation).

142   *stay :* await.
   convinces : defeats.

143 *great assay of art :* greatest efforts of medical skill.

145 *presently amend :* recover at once.

146 *the Evil.* The 'King's Evil' was scrofula, a form of tuberculosis. It was thought that the king had a heavenly gift for healing this disease, and it was also believed (see lines 155–6) that this power was hereditary.

148 *here-remain :* staying here.

149 *solicits heaven :* prays to God for this power.

150 *visited :* afflicted.

152 *mere :* complete.

153 *a golden stamp :* a special medal, stamped with the figure of St. Michael; monarchs before King James made the sign of the cross over the patient with this medal, but James simply hung it round their necks.

154 *'tis spoken :* it is said.

156 *healing benediction :* blessed gift of healing.
    virtue : power.

158 *sundry :* various.

160 Ross's clothes would indicate that he was Scottish.

161 *ever-gentle :* always noble.
    cousin : kinsman.

162 *betimes :* quickly.

163 *means :* circumstances.

164 Is Scotland still the same as it was?

165 *Almost . . . itself :* the people of Scotland are almost afraid to know each other.

166–7 No-one is ever seen to smile, except those who do not know what is going on.

The great assay of art; but, at his touch,
Such sanctity hath heaven given his hand,
145 They presently amend.

Malcolm   I thank you, doctor.
                    [*Exit* Doctor

Macduff
What's the disease he means?

Malcolm   'Tis call'd the Evil:
A most miraculous work in this good king,
Which often, since my here-remain in England,
I have seen him do. How he solicits heaven,
150 Himself best knows; but strangely-visited people,
All swoln and ulcerous, pitiful to the eye,
The mere despair of surgery, he cures,
Hanging a golden stamp about their necks,
Put on with holy prayers; and 'tis spoken,
155 To the succeeding royalty he leaves
The healing benediction. With this strange virtue,
He hath a heavenly gift of prophecy,
And sundry blessings hang about his throne,
That speak him full of grace.

                    Enter Ross
Macduff   See, who comes here?
Malcolm
160 My countryman; but yet I know him not.
Macduff
My ever-gentle cousin, welcome hither.
Malcolm
I know him now. Good God, betimes remove
The means that makes us strangers!
Ross   Sir, amen.
Macduff
Stands Scotland where it did?
Ross   Alas! poor country;
165 Almost afraid to know itself. It cannot
Be call'd our mother, but our grave; where nothing,
But who knows nothing, is once seen to smile;

169   *not mark'd :* unnoticed.

170   *A modern ecstasy :* a commonplace
       emotion.

170-1 Hardly anyone bothers to ask who
       is dead when they hear a funeral bell
       ('knell').

173   *or ere :* before.
       relation : tale.

174   *nice :* accurate.
       newest : latest.

175   A sad story that is one hour old
       causes the teller to be hissed at (because
       it is out of date).

176   *teems :* is stocked with.
       does : is.

180   *niggard :* miser.

182   *heavily :* sadly.

183   *out :* out in the field (fighting
       against Macbeth).

184   The rumour was the more
       confirmed in my belief.

185   *For that :* because.
       power : forces.
       a-foot : on the march.

186   *of :* to.
       eye : appearance (he speaks to
       Malcolm).

188   *doff :* cast off (like clothes).
       Be 't their comfort : may it be a
       comfort to them.

189   *Gracious England :* i.e. Edward the
       Confessor.

191   *older :* more experienced.

191-2 *none . . . out :* no soldier in
       Christendom is said to be.

Where sighs and groans and shrieks that rent the
       air
Are made, not mark'd; where violent sorrow seems
170 A modern ecstasy; the dead man's knell
Is there scarce ask'd for who; and good men's lives
Expire before the flowers in their caps,
Dying or ere they sicken.
    Macduff   O relation
Too nice, and yet too true!
    Malcolm   What's the newest grief?
    Ross
175 That of an hour's age doth hiss the speaker;
Each minute teems a new one.
    Macduff   How does my wife?
    Ross
Why, well.
    Macduff   And all my children?
    Ross   Well too.
    Macduff
The tyrant has not batter'd at their peace?
    Ross
No; they were well at peace when I did leave 'em.
    Macduff
180 Be not a niggard of your speech: how goes 't?
    Ross
When I came hither to transport the tidings,
Which I have heavily borne, there ran a rumour
Of many worthy fellows that were out;
Which was to my belief witness'd the rather
185 For that I saw the tyrant's power a-foot.
Now is the time of help; your eye in Scotland
Would create soldiers, make our women fight,
To doff their dire distresses.
    Malcolm   Be 't their comfort
We are coming thither. Gracious England hath
190 Lent us good Siward and ten thousand men—
An older and a better soldier none
That Christendom gives out.

193   *the like* : the same.
194   *would be* : ought to be.
195   *latch* : catch.

196   *a fee-grief* : a private grief.
197   *Due to* : owing to.

199   *Pertains* : belongs.

205   *the manner* : the way they were
      killed.
206   *quarry* : animals killed in a hunt.
      deer. There is a pun with 'dear'.

208   Macduff hides his face in his hat.

210   *Whispers* : whispers to.
      o'er-fraught : overloaded.

212   And I had to be away from there!

Ross   Would I could answer
This comfort with the like! But I have words
That would be howl'd out in the desert air,
195 Where hearing should not latch them.
      Macduff   What concern they?
The general cause? or is it a fee-grief
Due to some single breast?
      Ross   No mind that's honest
But in it shares some woe, though the main part
Pertains to you alone.
      Macduff   If it be mine
200 Keep it not from me; quickly let me have it.
      Ross
Let not your ears despise my tongue for ever,
Which shall possess them with the heaviest sound
That ever yet they heard.
      Macduff   Hum! I guess at it.
      Ross
Your castle is surpris'd; your wife and babes
205 Savagely slaughter'd; to relate the manner
Were, on the quarry of these murder'd deer,
To add the death of you.
      Malcolm   Merciful heaven!
What, man! ne'er pull your hat upon your brows;
Give sorrow words; the grief that does not speak
210 Whispers the o'er-fraught heart and bids it break.
      Macduff
My children too?
      Ross   Wife, children, servants, all
That could be found.
      Macduff   And I must be from thence!
My wife kill'd too?
      Ross   I have said.

216   *He ... children.* This may refer
to Malcolm (he would not speak so
unfeelingly if he were a father); or it
might refer to Macbeth.

218   *dam :* mother.

219   *fell :* cruel.
swoop : stroke (Macduff is still
thinking of Macbeth as a bird—
'hell-kite'—that 'swoops' down on its
prey).
Dispute : bear.

222   *cannot but remember :* cannot help
remembering.
such things : i.e. his wife and
children.

225   *struck for thee :* killed for your
faults.
Naught that I am : although I am
nothing.

226   *demerits :* failings.

228   *whetstone :* the stone used for
sharpening knives and swords.

229   *blunt ... it :* do not let your heart
become insensitive, but let it be angry.

230   *play ... eyes :* my eyes could play
the part of a woman (and weep).

231   *braggart :* boaster (who threatens
more than he can do).

232   *intermission :* interval (between
now and the time he sees Macbeth).
front to front : face to face.

234-5   If I let him escape, it will serve
me right if heaven forgives him too.

236   *power :* force (army).

237   We need nothing except to say
goodbye.

239   *instruments :* weapons. Malcolm
claims that the forces of good are
arming themselves to aid him, just as
Lady Macbeth called for the ministers
of evil to help her with the murder of
Duncan (*1*, 5, 47-9).
cheer : comfort.

Malcolm   Be comforted:
Let's make us medicine of our great revenge,
215 To cure this deadly grief.
    Macduff
He has no children. All my pretty ones?
Did you say all? O hell-kite! All?
What, all my pretty chickens and their dam
At one fell swoop?
    Malcolm   Dispute it like a man.
    Macduff
220 I shall do so;
But I must also feel it as a man:
I cannot but remember such things were,
That were most precious to me. Did heaven look on,
And would not take their part? Sinful Macduff!
225 They were all struck for thee. Naught that I am,
Not for their own demerits, but for mine,
Fell slaughter on their souls. Heaven rest them
    now.
    Malcolm
Be this the whetstone of your sword: let grief
Convert to anger; blunt not the heart, enrage it.
    Macduff
230 O, I could play the woman with mine eyes,
And braggart with my tongue. But, gentle heavens,
Cut short all intermission; front to front
Bring thou this fiend of Scotland and myself;
Within my sword's length set him; if he 'scape,
235 Heaven forgive him too!
    Malcolm   This tune goes manly.
Come, go we to the king; our power is ready;
Our lack is nothing but our leave. Macbeth
Is ripe for shaking, and the powers above
Put on their instruments. Receive what cheer you
    may;
240 The night is long that never finds the day.
                                        [*Exeunt*

Act 5

Act 5   scene 1

Lady Macbeth suffers from a guilty conscience. She walks in her sleep, and dreams that she and her husband are murdering King Duncan.

1   *watched*: stayed awake.

4   *the field*: i.e. the battlefield.

5   *night-gown*: dressing-gown.

6   *closet*: cupboard.

8   *fast*: sound.

9   *perturbation in nature*: upheaval in life.

10   *do . . . watching*: act as if she were awake.

11   *slumbery agitation*: activity whilst sleeping.

14   *report after her*: repeat behind her back.

15   *meet*: proper.

18   *guise*: appearance.

20   *close*: hidden.

Scene 1 *Dunsinane. A room in the castle*

A Doctor of Physic and a Waiting-Gentlewoman

Doctor
I have two nights watched with you, but can perceive no truth in your report. When was it she last walked?

Gentlewoman
Since his majesty went into the field, I have seen
5 her rise from her bed, throw her night-gown upon her, unlock her closet, take forth paper, fold it, write upon 't, read it, afterwards seal it, and again return to bed; yet all this while in a most fast sleep.

Doctor
A great perturbation in nature, to receive at once
10 the benefit of sleep and do the effects of watching! In this slumbery agitation, besides her walking and other actual performances, what, at any time, have you heard her say?

Gentlewoman
That, sir, which I will not report after her.

Doctor
15 You may to me, and 'tis most meet you should.

Gentlewoman
Neither to you nor any one, having no witness to confirm my speech.

Enter Lady Macbeth *with a candle*
Lo you! here she comes. This is her very guise; and, upon my life, fast asleep. Observe her; stand
20 close.

Doctor
How came she by that light?

Gentlewoman
Why, it stood by her: she has light by her continually; 'tis her command.

25   *sense :* understanding.

32   *set :* write.
33   *satisfy my remembrance :* confirm my
      memory.

36   *afeard :* afraid.
37   *none . . . account :* no one will be able
      to make us confess how we got this
      power.

44   *starting :* jumpiness.

45   *Go to :* Alas!

Doctor
You see, her eyes are open.
Gentlewoman
25 Ay, but their sense is shut.
Doctor
What is it she does now? Look, how she rubs her
hands.
Gentlewoman
It is an accustomed action with her, to seem thus
washing her hands. I have known her continue in
30 this a quarter of an hour.
Lady Macbeth
Yet here's a spot.
Doctor
Hark! she speaks. I will set down what comes from
her, to satisfy my remembrance the more strongly.
Lady Macbeth
Out, damned spot! out, I say! One; two: why, then
35 'tis time to do 't. Hell is murky! Fie, my lord—fie!
a soldier, and afeard? What need we fear who
knows it, when none can call our power to account?
Yet who would have thought the old man to have
had so much blood in him?
Doctor
40 Do you mark that?
Lady Macbeth
The Thane of Fife had a wife: where is she now?
What, will these hands ne'er be clean? No more
o' that, my lord, no more o' that: you mar all with
this starting.
Doctor
45 Go to, go to; you have known what you should not.
Gentlewoman
She has spoke what she should not, I am sure of
that: Heaven knows what she has known.
Lady Macbeth
Here's the smell of the blood still: all the perfumes
of Arabia will not sweeten this little hand. Oh!
50 oh! oh!

Doctor
What a sigh is there! The heart is sorely charged.

Gentlewoman
I would not have such a heart in my bosom for the dignity of the whole body.

Doctor
Well, well, well.

Gentlewoman
55 Pray God it be, sir.

Doctor
This disease is beyond my practice: yet I have known those which have walked in their sleep who have died holily in their beds.

Lady Macbeth
Wash your hands, put on your night-gown; look
60 not so pale. I tell you yet again, Banquo's buried; he cannot come out on 's grave.

Doctor
Even so?

Lady Macbeth
To bed, to bed: there's knocking at the gate. Come, come, come, come, give me your hand. What's
65 done cannot be undone. To bed, to bed, to bed.
[*Exit*

Doctor
Will she go now to bed?

Gentlewoman
Directly.

Doctor
Foul whisperings are abroad. Unnatural deeds
Do breed unnatural troubles; infected minds
70 To their deaf pillows will discharge their secrets.
More needs she the divine than the physician.
God, God forgive us all! Look after her;
Remove from her the means of all annoyance,
And still keep eyes upon her. So, good-night:
75 My mind she has mated, and amaz'd my sight.
I think, but dare not speak.

Gentlewoman   Good-night, good doctor.
[*Exeunt*

---

51   *sorely charged :* grievously burdened.

56   *beyond my practice :* too serious for me to treat.

61   *on 's :* of his.

68   *whisperings :* rumours.
     abroad : about, at large.
70   *discharge :* confide.
71   *divine :* priest.

73   *means of all annoyance :* anything she might use to harm herself.
74   *still :* always.
75   *mated :* bewildered.

Act 5   scene 2

A section of the army marches towards Dunsinane. The leaders discuss their enemy, Macbeth, who is showing signs of panic.

sd   *colours*: regimental banners.

3   *Revenges*: desire for revenge.

3-5   Their causes are powerful enough to rouse ('Excite') a dead ('mortified') man to come to the bloodshed and answer the call to arms ('alarm').

8   *file*: list.

10   *unrough*: beardless.

11   Show that they have now reached manhood.

15-16   These lines could mean *either* 'He cannot discipline his rebellious ("distemper'd") kingdom', *or* 'He cannot restrain his own diseased ("distemper'd") passions'.

18   Now every minute more men revolt from him, and this rebukes him for his own rebellion.

19-20   They obey him because he is their commander, not because they love him.

23   *pester'd senses*: troubled nerves. *to recoil and start*: to be jumpy.

24-5   His whole being is revolted by itself.

Scene 2 *Countryside near Dunsinane*

> *Enter, with drum and colours,* Menteith, Caithness, Angus, Lennox, *and* Soldiers

Menteith
The English power is near, led on by Malcolm,
His uncle Siward, and the good Macduff.
Revenges burn in them; for their dear causes
Would to the bleeding and the grim alarm
5 Excite the mortified man.
Angus   Near Birnam wood
Shall we well meet them; that way are they coming
Caithness
Who knows if Donalbain be with his brother?
Lennox
For certain, sir, he is not: I have a file
Of all the gentry: there is Siward's son,
10 And many unrough youths that even now
Protest their first of manhood.
Menteith   What does the tyrant
Caithness
Great Dunsinane he strongly fortifies.
Some say he's mad; others, that lesser hate him
Do call it valiant fury; but, for certain,
15 He cannot buckle his distemper'd cause
Within the belt of rule.
Angus   Now does he feel
His secret murders sticking on his hands;
Now minutely revolts upbraid his faith-breach;
Those he commands move only in command,
20 Nothing in love; now does he feel his title
Hang loose about him, like a giant's robe
Upon a dwarfish thief.
Menteith   Who then shall blame
His pester'd senses to recoil and start,
When all that is within him does condemn
25 Itself for being there?

Caithness   Well, march we on,
To give obedience where 'tis truly ow'd;
Meet we the medicine of the sickly weal,
And with him pour we in our country's purge,
Each drop of us.
Lennox   Or so much as it needs
30 To dew the sovereign flower and drown the weeds.
Make we our march towards Birnam.

                                [Exeunt, marching

Scene 3 *Dunsinane. A room in the castle*

Enter Macbeth, Doctor, *and* Attendants
    Macbeth
Bring me no more reports; let them fly all:
Till Birnam wood remove to Dunsinane
I cannot taint with fear. What's the boy Malcolm?
Was he not born of woman? The spirits that know
5 All mortal consequences have pronounc'd me thus:
'Fear not, Macbeth; no man that's born of woman
Shall e'er have power upon thee.' Then fly, false thanes,
And mingle with the English epicures:
The mind I sway by, and the heart I bear
10 Shall never sag with doubt nor shake with fear.

Enter a Servant
The devil damn thee black, thou cream-fac'd loon!
Where gott'st thou that goose look?
    Servant
There is ten thousand—
    Macbeth   Geese, villain?
    Servant   Soldiers, sir.
    Macbeth
Go, prick thy face, and over-red thy fear,
15 Thou lily-liver'd boy. What soldiers, patch?
Death of thy soul! those linen cheeks of thine
Are counsellors to fear. What soldiers, whey-face?
    Servant
The English force, so please you.

---

27 *the medicine* : the doctor (i.e. Malcolm).
    weal : land.
28 Let us, with Malcolm, pour out every drop of our blood to cleanse our country. (A widely-prescribed treatment for diseases was blood-letting—drawing off some of the patient's blood.)
30 *dew* : water.

Act 5   scene 3
Macbeth tries to comfort himself by recalling the witches' prophecies as he is told of the approaching armies. He discusses his wife's illness with the Doctor, and then goes off to battle.

1 *them* : i.e. the thanes.
2 *remove* : moves.
3 *taint* : go rotten.
    mortal consequences : human causes and effects.
    have pronounc'd me : have spoken about me.

8 *English epicures* : soft-living English.
9 *sway* : rule myself.

11 *loon* : fool.

14 *over-red thy fear* : colour your white face (white through fear) red with the blood from the pricks.
15 *lily-liver'd* : coward—because the blood had drained from his liver, the seat of courage, and left it white like a lily.
    patch : clown.
16 *linen* : i.e. white.
17 *counsellors* : persuaders.
    whey : the thin white liquid that is left when milk has curdled.

Macbeth
Take thy face hence.   [*Exit* Servant
Seyton! I am sick at heart

20 When I behold—Seyton, I say!—This push
Will cheer me ever or disseat me now.
I have liv'd long enough: my way of life
Is fall'n into the sere, the yellow leaf;
And that which should accompany old age,
25 As honour, love, obedience, troops of friends,
I must not look to have; but, in their stead,
Curses, not loud but deep, mouth-honour, breath,
Which the poor heart would fain deny, and dare
    not.
Seyton!

Enter Seyton

Seyton
30 What is your gracious pleasure?
      Macbeth   What news more?
Seyton
All is confirm'd, my lord, which was reported.
      Macbeth
I'll fight till from my bones my flesh be hack'd.
Give me my armour.
      Seyton   'Tis not needed yet.
      Macbeth
I'll put it on.
35 Send out more horses, skirr the country round;
Hang those that talk of fear. Give me mine armour.
How does your patient, doctor?
      Doctor   Not so sick, my lord,
As she is troubled with thick-coming fancies,
That keep her from her rest.
      Macbeth   Cure her of that.
40 Canst thou not minister to a mind diseas'd,
Pluck from the memory a rooted sorrow,
Raze out the written troubles of the brain,
And with some sweet oblivious antidote
Cleanse the stuff'd bosom of that perilous stuff
45 Which weighs upon the heart?

---

20 *behold*. He does not complete the sentence.
    push : attack.
21 *cheer* : comfort; but there is also a pun with 'chair' meaning 'enthrone'.
    disseat : de-throne.
22 *my way of life* : the course of my life.
23 *the sere* : the withered state.
27 *mouth-honour* : lip-service.
28 *fain deny* : wish to withold.

35 *skirr* : scour, move swiftly.

38 *thick-coming* : crowding in on each other.

40 *minister to* : treat.
41 *rooted* : deeply embedded.
42 *Raze* : erase.
    written : imprinted.
43 *oblivious* : causing forgetfulness.
44 *stuff'd bosom* : burdened heart.
45 *weighs upon* : distresses.

Doctor   Therein the patient
Must minister to himself.

> **47** *I'll none of it :* I won't have anything to do with it (because it is useless).

Macbeth
Throw physic to the dogs; I'll none of it.
Come, put mine armour on; give me my staff.
Seyton, send out.—Doctor, the thanes fly from
  me.—

> **50** *dispatch :* get on with it!
> *cast :* analyse.
> **51** *water :* urine.
> **52** *pristine :* as good as new.
> **53-4** I would praise you so loudly that my praises would echo and re-echo.
> **54** *Pull 't off :* Some piece of armour does not fit properly, and he orders Seyton to take it off and (line 58) bring it after him.
> **55** Rhubarb and senna are both 'purgative' (laxative) drugs.
> **57** *preparation :* i.e. for war.

50 Come, sir, dispatch.—If thou couldst, doctor, cast
The water of my land, find her disease,
And purge it to a sound and pristine health,
I would applaud thee to the very echo,
That should applaud again.—Pull 't off, I say.—
55 What rhubarb, senna, or what purgative drug
Would scour these English hence? Hear'st thou of
  them?

Doctor
Ay, my good lord; your royal preparation
Makes us hear something.

> **59** *bane :* destruction.

Macbeth   Bring it after me.
I will not be afraid of death and bane
60 Till Birnam forest come to Dunsinane.

> **61** *clear :* free.
> **62** *Profit :* Doctors were noted for avarice.

Doctor
[*Aside*] Were I from Dunsinane away and clear,
Profit again should hardly draw me here.   [*Exeunt*

> **Act 5   scene 4**
> Malcolm and his soldiers draw closer to Dunsinane.

Scene 4 *Near Birnam Wood*

> **2** *chambers :* bedrooms—i.e. where we can sleep in safety.
> *nothing :* not at all.

Enter, with drum and colours, Malcolm,
Old Siward *and his* Son, Macduff,
Menteith, Caithness, Angus, Lennox,
Ross, *and* Soldiers, *marching*

Malcolm
Cousins, I hope the days are near at hand
That chambers will be safe.

Menteith   We doubt it nothing.

Siward
What wood is this before us?

Menteith
The wood of Birnam.

Malcolm

5 Let every soldier hew him down a bough
And bear 't before him: thereby shall we shadow
The numbers of our host, and make discovery
Err in report of us.

Soldiers   It shall be done.

Siward

We learn no other but the confident tyrant
10 Keeps still in Dunsinane, and will endure
Our setting down before 't.

Malcolm   'Tis his main hope;
For where there is advantage to be gone,
Both more and less have given him the revolt,
And none serve with him but constrained things
15 Whose hearts are absent too.

Macduff   Let our just censures
Attend the true event, and put we on
Industrious soldiership.

Siward   The time approaches
That will with due decision make us know
What we shall say we have, and what we owe.
20 Thoughts speculative their unsure hopes relate,
But certain issue strokes must arbitrate,
Towards which advance the war.

                                    [*Exeunt, marching*

Scene 5 *Inside the castle*

Enter, with a drum and colours, Macbeth,
Seyton, *and* Soldiers

Macbeth

Hang out our banners on the outward walls;
The cry is still, 'They come'. Our castle's strength
Will laugh a siege to scorn; here let them lie
Till famine and the ague eat them up;
5 Were they not forc'd with those that should be ours,

6-7   *shadow . . . host :* conceal the size of our army.
7-8   *make . . . us :* make those who spy on us give a false report.

9   *no other :* nothing else.
10   *endure :* allow.
11   *our setting down :* i.e. in a siege.

12   *advantage to be gone :* opportunity to escape.
13   *more and less :* high and low in rank.
    given . . . revolt : rebelled against him.
14   *constrained things :* miserable conscripts.
15-16   *Let . . . event :* let us wait to give an opinion until after the event.
18   *due :* proper (because the decision will be made by the result of the battle).
19   What we can claim to possess, and what we lack.
20-1   Speculation about what will happen is based on uncertain hopes, but actual fighting ('strokes') must decide ('arbitrate') the outcome ('issue') and make it certain. (Like Macduff, Siward warns Malcolm not to be too optimistic.)
22   *advance :* carry on with.

Act 5   scene 5

The battle is at its height when Seyton brings news to Macbeth that his wife has just died. Macbeth does not grieve, because he feels that life is meaningless. A Messenger tells him that Birnam Wood is moving towards the castle.

4   *ague :* fever.
5   *forc'd :* reinforced.

6 *dareful* : defiantly.

We might have met them dareful, beard to beard,
And beat them backward home.
                              [*A cry of women within*
                              What is that noise?

Seyton
It is the cry of women, my good lord.   [*Exit*

Macbeth
I have almost forgot the taste of fears.

10 *cool'd* : frozen.
11 *night-shriek* : cry at night.
    fell : fleece, scalp.
12 *dismal treatise* : frightening story.
13 *As* : as if.
14 *Direness* : horror.
15 *Cannot . . . me* : can never alarm me.

10 The time has been my senses would have cool'd
To hear a night-shriek, and my fell of hair
Would at a dismal treatise rouse and stir
As life were in 't. I have supp'd full with horrors;
Direness, familiar to my slaughterous thoughts,
15 Cannot once start me.

                    Enter Seyton
                              Wherefore was that cry?

Seyton
The queen, my lord, is dead.

Macbeth
She should have died hereafter;
There would have been a time for such a word.
To-morrow, and to-morrow, and to-morrow,

17 She would have died at some time
    or other.
18 The word would have to be spoken
    at some time.
20 One day creeps after another at
    this trivial rate.
21 Until the very end of time—the
    last syllable written in the book.
22-3 Every day that has passed has done
    no more than give light to fools on
    their way to death.
23 *candle* : i.e. Life.

20 Creeps in this petty pace from day to day,
To the last syllable of recorded time;
And all our yesterdays have lighted fools
The way to dusty death. Out, out, brief candle!
Life's but a walking shadow, a poor player
25 That struts and frets his hour upon the stage,
And then is heard no more; it is a tale
Told by an idiot, full of sound and fury,
Signifying nothing.

                    Enter a Messenger
Thou com'st to use thy tongue; thy story quickly.

Messenger
30 Gracious my lord,
I should report that which I say I saw,
But know not how to do it.

31 *should* : ought to.
    I say I saw : I declare I saw.

Macbeth   Well, say, sir.

Messenger
As I did stand my watch upon the hill,

33 *watch* : guard.

34 *anon :* suddenly.

I look'd toward Birnam, and anon, methought,
35 The wood began to move.
    Macbeth   Liar and slave!
    Messenger
Let me endure your wrath if 't be not so:
Within this three mile you may see it coming;
I say, a moving grove.
    Macbeth   If thou speak'st false,
Upon the next tree shalt thou hang alive,

40 *cling :* shrink up.
    sooth : the truth.
41 *as much :* the same.
42 *pull in resolution :* check my determination.
43 *equivocation :* double dealing.
44 Whose lies become truths.

40 Till famine cling thee; if thy speech be sooth,
I care not if thou dost for me as much.
I pull in resolution, and begin
To doubt the equivocation of the fiend
That lies like truth; 'Fear not, till Birnam wood
45 Do come to Dunsinane', and now a wood
Comes toward Dunsinane. Arm, arm, and out!

47 *avouches :* affirms.
48 I can neither escape nor stay here.
49 *the sun :* i.e. life.
50 *estate o' the world :* the whole creation.
51 *wrack :* wreck.
52 *harness :* armour.

If this which he avouches does appear,
There is nor flying hence, nor tarrying here.
I 'gin to be aweary of the sun,
50 And wish the estate o' the world were now undone.
Ring the alarum-bell! Blow, wind! come, wrack!
At least we'll die with harness on our back.
                            [*Exeunt*

Act 5   scene 6
Battle is commenced.

Scene 6 *A plain before the castle*

        Enter, with drum and colours, Malcolm,
        Old Siward, Macduff, *and their Army,*
        with boughs
    Malcolm
Now near enough; your leafy screens throw down,

2 *show like those you are :* appear as yourselves (i.e. soldiers).

And show like those you are. You, worthy uncle,
Shall, with my cousin, your right noble son,
Lead our first battle; worthy Macduff and we
5 Shall take upon 's what else remains to do,
According to our order.

6 *order :* plan of campaign.

    Siward   Fare you well.
Do we but find the tyrant's power tonight,

7 *power :* army.

Let us be beaten, if we cannot fight.
    Macduff
Make all our trumpets speak; give them all breath,

10 *harbingers :* heralds.

10 Those clamorous harbingers of blood and death.
                            [*Exeunt*

Act 5   scene 7

The battle continues throughout this scene. Macbeth meets young Siward, and kills him. Macduff hurries across the stage in search of Macbeth. They fight. Victory is proclaimed, and Malcolm is king.

1   *tied me to a stake.* A bear was tied to a post and attacked by dogs in the sport of 'bear-baiting'.

Scene 7 *Another part of the plain*

Alarums. Enter Macbeth

Macbeth
They have tied me to a stake; I cannot fly,
But bear-like I must fight the course. What's he
That was not born of woman? Such a one
Am I to fear, or none.

Enter Young Siward

Young Siward
5 What is thy name?

   Macbeth   Thou'lt be afraid to hear it.

   Young Siward
No; though thou call'st thyself a hotter name
Than any is in hell.

   Macbeth   My name's Macbeth.

   Young Siward
The devil himself could not pronounce a title
More hateful to mine ear.

   Macbeth   No, nor more fearful.

Young Siward

10 Thou liest, abhorred tyrant; with my sword
I'll prove the lie thou speak'st.
                                    [*They fight and Young* Siward *is slain*
Macbeth   Thou wast born of woman:
But swords I smile at, weapons laugh to scorn,
Brandish'd by man that's of a woman born.   [*Exit*

Alarums. Enter Macduff

Macduff
That way the noise is. Tyrant, show thy face:
15 If thou be'st slain and with no stroke of mine,
My wife and children's ghosts will haunt me still.
I cannot strike at wretched kerns, whose arms
Are hir'd to bear their staves: either thou, Macbeth,
Or else my sword with an unbatter'd edge
20 I sheathe again undeeded. There thou shouldst be;
By this great clatter, one of greatest note
Seems bruited. Let me find him, fortune!
And more I beg not.   [*Exit. Alarums*

Enter Malcolm *and Old* Siward

Siward
This way, my lord; the castle's gently render'd:
25 The tyrant's people on both sides do fight;
The noble thanes do bravely in the war;
The day almost itself professes yours,
And little is to do.
Malcolm   We have met with foes
That strike beside us.
Siward   Enter, sir, the castle.
                                    [*Exeunt. Alarums*

Enter Macbeth

Macbeth
30 Why should I play the Roman fool, and die
On mine own sword? whiles I see lives, the gashes
Do better upon them.

Enter Macduff

Macduff   Turn, hell-hound, turn!
Macbeth
Of all men else I have avoided thee:
But get thee back, my soul is too much charg'd
35 With blood of thine already.

11   *prove the lie*: prove it to be a lie.

16   *still*: for ever.
17   *kerns*: mercenaries (see note to
1, 2, 13).
18   *staves*: spear-shafts.
20   *undeeded*: not having performed any
deeds.
21   *note*: importance.
22   *bruited*: reported.

24   *gently render'd*: peaceably
surrendered.

27   You have almost won the day.

29   *strike beside us*: fight on our side.

30   *Roman*. The Romans thought it
dishonourable to be captured, and
when they knew they were defeated
they committed suicide.

34   *charg'd*: guilty.

Macduff   I have no words;
My voice is in my sword, thou bloodier villain
Than terms can give thee out!   [*They fight*
  Macbeth   Thou losest labour:
As easy may'st thou the intrenchant air
With thy keen sword impress, as make me bleed:
40 Let fall thy blade on vulnerable crests;
I bear a charmed life, which must not yield
To one of woman born.
  Macduff   Despair thy charm;
And let the angel whom thou still hast serv'd
Tell thee, Macduff was from his mother's womb
45 Untimely ripp'd.
  Macbeth
Accursed be that tongue that tells me so,
For it hath cow'd my better part of man:
And be these juggling fiends no more believ'd,
That palter with us in a double sense;
50 That keep the word of promise to our ear,
And break it to our hope. I'll not fight with thee.
  Macduff
Then yield thee, coward,
And live to be the show and gaze o' the time:
We'll have thee, as our rarer monsters are,
55 Painted upon a pole, and underwrit,
'Here may you see the tyrant.'
  Macbeth   I will not yield,
To kiss the ground before young Malcolm's feet,
And to be baited with the rabble's curse.
Though Birnam wood be come to Dunsinane,
60 And thou oppos'd, being of no woman born,
Yet I will try the last. Before my body
I throw my warlike shield: lay on, Macduff,
And damn'd be him that first cries, 'Hold, enough!'
                             [*Exeunt, fighting*

*Retreat. Flourish. Enter, with drum and
colours,* Malcolm, *Old* Siward, Ross,
Thanes, *and* Soldiers
  Malcolm
I would the friends we miss were safe arriv'd.

---

37   *Than . . . out :* than words can say.

38   *intrenchant :* incapable of being cut, invulnerable.
39   *impress :* make an impression on.

41   *must not :* is not destined to be.

42   *Despair :* despair of.

45   *Untimely :* prematurely; Macduff was delivered by a caesarean operation.

47   *cow'd . . . man :* subdued my spirit.
48   *juggling :* deceptive (they played with words as a juggler plays with balls).
49   *palter :* trifle.
    in a double sense : using words with two meanings, ambiguously.
50-1 Keep their promise by the sound of it, but break it when we do not get what we hoped for.
53   *show . . . time :* spectacle of the age.
55   Painted on a sign which is hung from a pole.
    underwrit : written underneath.

58   *baited :* taunted.

60   *oppos'd :* fighting against me.
61   *try the last :* fight to the end.

63sd *Retreat. Flourish :* trumpets give a call that signifies surrender; then other trumpets (Malcolm's) sound the call of triumph.

64   *we miss :* who are absent.

65   *go off :* be killed.
      by these : judging by these men I
      see here.

68   *soldier's debt :* i.e. he has been
      killed in action.

71   In the post where he fought without
      flinching.
73   *brought off the field :* his body has
      been carried from the battlefield.
73-5 You must not mourn for him as
      much as he deserves, because then you
      would never stop mourning.
75   *before :* on the front of his body (he
      was not running away when he was
      killed).
76   I give him as a soldier to God.

77   *hairs.* Siward makes a brave pun
      on 'heirs'.
79   *his knell is knoll'd :* his funeral bell
      has been rung (and there is no more
      to say).
81   *parted :* died.
      score : debts.

84   *time :* age.
85   *pearl :* jewels (i.e. the nobles).
86-7 They salute you in their hearts as
      I do, and I want them to say aloud
      with me.

Siward
65 Some must go off; and yet, by these I see,
    So great a day as this is cheaply bought.
        Malcolm
    Macduff is missing, and your noble son.
        Ross
    Your son, my lord, has paid a soldier's debt:
    He only liv'd but till he was a man;
70 The which no sooner had his prowess confirm'd
    In the unshrinking station where he fought,
    But like a man he died.
        Siward   Then he is dead?
        Ross
    Ay, and brought off the field. Your cause of sorrow
    Must not be measur'd by his worth, for then
75 It hath no end.
        Siward   Had he his hurts before?
        Ross
    Ay, on the front.
        Siward   Why then, God's soldier be he!
    Had I as many sons as I have hairs,
    I would not wish them to a fairer death:
    And so, his knell is knoll'd.
        Malcolm   He's worth more sorrow,
80 And that I'll spend for him.
        Siward   He's worth no more;
    They say he parted well, and paid his score:
    And so, God be with him! Here comes newer
        comfort.

            Enter Macduff, *with* Macbeth's *head*
        Macduff
    Hail, king! for so thou art. Behold, where stands
    The usurper's cursed head: the time is free.
85 I see thee compass'd with thy kingdom's pearl,
    That speak my salutation in their minds;
    Whose voices I desire aloud with mine:
    Hail, King of Scotland!
        All   Hail, King of Scotland!
                                        [*Flourish*

90 *reckon . . . loves* : repay each one of you individually for your loyalty.
91 *even* : equal (in obligation).

94 *would be* : ought to be.
planted . . . time : started now, just as a new age has begun.

97 *Producing forth* : bringing out.
ministers : agents.

99 *by self and violent hands* : by her own violent hands.
100 *what needful else* : whatever else is necessary.
101 *calls upon us* : demands our attention.
grace of Grace : grace of God.
102 *in measure, time, and place* : in the proper order, at the right time, and in the proper place. Malcolm has brought harmony back to Scotland.

Malcolm
We shall not spend a large expense of time
90 Before we reckon with your several loves,
And make us even with you. My thanes and
  kinsmen,
Henceforth be earls, the first that ever Scotland
In such an honour nam'd. What's more to do,
Which would be planted newly with the time—
95 As calling home our exil'd friends abroad
That fled the snares of watchful tyranny;
Producing forth the cruel ministers
Of this dead butcher and his fiend-like queen,
Who, as 'tis thought, by self and violent hands
100 Took off her life—this, and what needful else
That calls upon us, by the grace of Grace,
We will perform in measure, time, and place.
So, thanks to all at once, and to each one,
Whom we invite to see us crown'd at Scone.
                              [*Flourish. Exeunt*

Macbeth: The source

Shakespeare's main source for *Macbeth* was *The Chronicles of Scotland*, which was compiled by Raphael Holinshed in 1577. These passages are extracts from the *Chronicles*, where Shakespeare found the complete outline of Macbeth's career, from his first encounter with the witches until his death at the hands of Macduff. Details of the murder of Duncan come from Holinshed's account of the killing of an earlier Scottish king, King Duff, who was also murdered by one of his subjects, the trusted Donwald. The spelling and punctuation have been modernized; dots (. . .) indicate that something has been missed out. In order to make a continuous narrative I have sometimes inserted words; these are indicated by the square brackets — [ ].

It fortuned as Macbeth and Banquo journeyed towards Forres . . . there met them three women in strange and wild apparel . . . The first of them spake and said, 'All hail, Macbeth, Thane of Glamis.' (For he had lately entered into that dignity and office by the death of his father Sinel.) The second of them said, 'All hail, Macbeth, Thane of Cawdor.' But the third said "All hail, Macbeth, that hereafter shalt be King of Scotland.'

Then Banquo: 'What manner of women' (said he) 'are you, that seem so little favourable unto me, whereas to my fellow here, besides high offices, ye assign also the Kingdom, appointing further nothing for me at all?'

'Yes' (says the first of them) 'we promise greater benefits unto thee than unto him, for he shall reign indeed, but with an unlucky end; neither shall he leave any issue behind him to succeed in his place, where contrarily thou indeed shall not reign at all, but of thee those shall be born which shall govern the Scottish Kingdom by long order of continual descent.'

Herewith the aforesaid women vanished immediately out of their sight . . . The common opinion was that these women were either the weird sisters . . . or else some nymphs or fairies . . .

Shortly after, the Thane of Cawdor being condemned at Forres of treason against the king committed, his lands, livings and offices were given of the king's liberality to Macbeth.

The same night after, at supper, Banquo jested with him and

said, 'Now, Macbeth, thou has obtained those things which the two
former sisters prophesied, there remaineth only for thee to
purchase that which the third said should come to pass.'

Whereupon Macbeth, revolving the thing in his mind, began
even then to devise how he might attain to the kingdom; but yet he
thought with himself that he must tarry a time, which should
advance him thereto (by the divine providence) as it had come to
pass in his former preferment. But shortly after it chanced that
King Duncan, having two sons . . . he made the elder of them
called Malcolm, Prince of Cumberland, as it were thereby to
appoint him his successor in the kingdom immediately after his
decease. Macbeth [was] sore troubled therewith [and] he began to
take counsel how he might usurp the kingdom by force . . .

The words of the three sisters . . . greatly encouraged him
hereunto, but specially his wife lay sore upon him to attempt the
thing, as she that was very ambitious, burning in unquenchable
desire to bear the name of queen. At length therefore . . . he slew
the king . . . [and then] he caused himself to be proclaimed king,
and forthwith went unto Scone, where . . . he received the investi-
ture of the kingdom according to the accustomed manner.

Malcolm . . . and Donald Bane, the sons of King Duncan, for
fear of their lives (which they might well know that Macbeth would
seek to bring to an end for his more sure confirmation in the estate)
fled into Cumberland, where Malcolm remained, till time that
[King] Edward . . . received [him] by way of most friendly
entertainment; but Donald passed over into Ireland where he was
tenderly cherished by the king of that land . . .

Macbeth govern[ed] the realm for a space of ten years in equal
justice . . . [but then] he began to show what he was . . . For the
prick of conscience . . . caused him ever to fear, lest he should be
served by the same cup as he had administered to his predecessor.

The words also of the three weird sisters would not out of his
mind, which as they had promised him the kingdom, so likewise
did they promise it at the same time unto the heirs of Banquo. He
willed, therefore, the same Banquo, with his son named Fleance, to
come to [a] supper that he had prepared for them — which was
indeed, as he had devised, present death at the hands of certain
murderers. [He had hired these men] to execute that deed,
appointing them to meet with that same Banquo and his son
without the palace, as they returned to their lodgings, and there to
slay them . . . it chanced yet by benefit of the dark night, that
although the father were slain, the son . . . escaped that danger . . .

After the contrived slaughter of Banquo, nothing prospered

with the foresaid Macbeth: for in manner every man began to doubt his own life . . . And even as there were many that stood in fear of him, so likewise stood he in fear of many . . .

[Macbeth] had learned of certain wizards . . . that he ought to take heed of Macduff, who in time to come should seek to destroy him. And surely hereupon had he put Macduff to death, but that a certain witch, whom he had in great trust, had told [him] that he should never be slain with man born of any woman, nor vanquished till the wood of Birnam came in[to] the castle of Dunsinane. By this prophecy Macbeth put all fear out of his heart, supposing that he might do what he would . . .

At length Macduff, to avoid peril of life, purposed with himself to pass into England, to procure Malcolm to claim the crown of Scotland. But this was not so secretly devised by Macduff, but that Macbeth had knowledge given him thereof . . . for Macbeth had in every nobleman's house one sly fellow or other in fee with him, to reveal all that was said or done within the same . . . Immediately then, being advertised whereabout Macduff went, he came hastily with a great power unto Fife, and forthwith besieged the castle where Macduff dwelt, trusting to have found him therein . . . Macbeth most cruelly caused the wife and children of Macduff, with all other whom he found in that castle, to be slain. Also he confiscated the goods of Macduff [and] proclaimed him traitor . . .

But Macduff was already escaped out of danger and gotten into England . . . [and] at his coming unto Malcolm, he declared into what great misery the estate of Scotland was brought, by the detestable cruelties exercised by the tyrant Macbeth.

Malcolm, hearing Macduff's words . . . fetched a deep sigh. [Macduff urged Malcolm to return and claim the crown of Scotland, but,] though Malcolm was very sorrowful for the oppression of his countrymen the Scots, in manner as Macduff had declared, yet doubting whether he would come as one that meant unfeignedly as he spake, or else as sent from Macbeth to betray him, he thought to have some further trial, and thereupon dissembling his mind at the first, he answered as follows:

'I am truly very sorry for the misery chanced to my country of Scotland, but though I have never so great affection to relieve the same, I am nothing meet thereto. First, such immoderate lust and voluptuous sensuality . . . followeth me, that if I were made King of Scots, I should seek to deflower your maids and matrons, in such wise that mine intemperance should be no more importable unto you than the bloody tyranny of Macbeth now is.' Hereunto Macduff answered, 'This surely is a very evil fault, for many noble princes and kings have lost both lives and kingdoms for the same; nevertheless, there are women ennow in Scotland . . .'

Then said Malcolm, 'I am also the most avaricious creature on the earth, so that if I were king, I should seek so many ways to get lands and goods, that I would slay the most part of all the nobles of Scotland to the end . . . that I might enjoy their lands, goods, and possessions . . .' Macduff to this made answer, how it was a far worse fault than the other: for avarice is the root of all mischief . . . 'Yet notwithstanding, follow my counsel, and take upon thee the crown. There is gold and riches enough in Scotland to satisfy thy greedy desire.'

Then said Malcolm again, 'I am further inclined to dissimulation, telling of leasings and all other kinds of deceit . . . Then sith there is nothing that more becometh a prince than constancy, verity, truth, and justice, with the other laudable fellowship of those fair and noble virtues . . . you see how unable I am to govern any province or region . . .'

Then said Macduff, "This is the worst of all, and there I leave thee, and therefore say, "Oh ye unhappy and miserable Scottishmen . . . ye have one cursed and wicked tyrant that now reigneth over you, without any right or title . . . The other, that hath the right to the crown, is . . . nothing worthy to enjoy it ever"' . . .

At the last, when he was ready to depart, Malcolm took him by the sleeve and said, 'Be of good comfort, Macduff, for I have none of these vices before remembered, but have jested with thee in this manner only to prove thy mind. For diverse times heretofore hath Macbeth sought by this manner of means to bring me into his hands . . .'

[Then Macduff returned to Scotland, and called the nobles of the realm to assist Malcolm to reclaim the throne.]

In the meantime, Malcolm purchased such favour at King Edward's hands, that old Siward, Earl of Northumberland, was appointed, with ten thousand men, to go with him into Scotland to support him in this enterprise for recovery of his right . . . After that Macbeth perceived his enemies' power to increase . . . he recoiled back into Fife, there purposing to abide in camp fortified at the castle of Dunsinane, and to fight with his enemies if they meant to pursue him . . . He had such confidence in his prophecies, that he believed that he should never be vanquished, till Birnam Wood be brought to Dunsinane, nor yet to be slain with any man that should be or was born of any woman.

Malcolm, following hastily after Macbeth, came the night before the battle unto Birnam Wood, and when his army had rested a while there to refresh them, he commanded every man to get a bough of some tree or other of that wood in his hand, as big as he might bear, and to march forth therewith in such wise that on the next morrow they might come closely and without sight in this manner within view of his enemies.

On the morrow, when Macbeth beheld them coming in this sort, [he] first marvelled what the matter meant, but in the end remembered himself that the prophecy which he had heard long time before that time, of the coming of Birnam Wood to Dunsinane Castle was likely to be fulfilled. Nevertheless, he brought his men in order of battle, and exhorted them to do valiantly. Howbeit, his enemies had scarcely cast from them their boughs when Macbeth, perceiving their numbers, betook him straight to flight . . .

[Macduff pursued Macbeth, who challenged him], saying, 'Thou traitor, what meaneth it that thou shouldst thus in vain follow me, that am not appointed to be slain by any creature that is born of a woman. Come on, therefore . . .' But Macduff . . . answered (with his naked sword in his hand), saying, 'It is true, Macbeth . . . for I am even he that thy wizards have told thee of, who was never born of my mother, but ripped out of her womb.' Therewithal he stepped unto [Macbeth], and slew him in the place. Then cutting his head from his shoulders he set it upon a pole and brought it unto Malcolm.

Malcolm . . . thus recovering the realm . . . was crowned at Scone . . . Immediately after his coronation, he called a parliament . . . in which he rewarded them in lands and in livings that had assisted him against Macbeth . . . He created many earls . . . [and] these were the first earls that have ever been heard of amongst the Scottishmen . . .

Earl Siward [had] sent his son [into Scotland] with an army to conquer the land, whose hap was there to be slain. When his father heard the news he demanded whether he received the wounds whereof he died in the fore-part of his body, or in the hinder-part: and when it was told him that he received it in the fore-part, 'I rejoice' (saith he) 'even with all my heart, for I would not wish either to my son nor to my self any other kind of death.'

Donwald murders King Duff.

[After some of his kinsmen had been put to death for treason, Donwald, the 'captain of the castle' at Forres], conceived such an inward malice toward the king . . . [and] through setting of his wife . . . he found means to murder the king within the aforesaid castle of Forres . . . For the king, being in that country, was accustomed to lie most commonly within the same castle, having special trust in Donwald, as a man whom he never suspected . . .

[Donwald still held a grudge against the King], which his wife, perceiving, ceased not to travail with him until she understood the cause of his displeasure. Which at length when she had learned by his own relation, she, as one that bear no less malice in her heart towards the king . . . counselled him . . . to make him away, and showed him the means whereby he might soonest accomplish it. Donwald thus being the more kindled in wrath by the words of his wife, determined to follow her advice in the execution of so heinous an act. Whereupon devising with himself for a while, which way he might best accomplish his accursed intent, [he] at length got opportunity, and sped his purpose as followeth.

It chanced that the king, upon the day before he purposed to depart forth of the castle . . . called such afore him as had faithfully served him in pursuit and apprehension of the rebels; and, giving them hearty thanks, he bestowed sundry honourable gifts amongst them. Of the which number Donwald was one, as he that had been ever accounted a most faithful servant to the king.

At length . . . he got him into his privy chamber, only with two of his chamberlains. [These men], having brought [the king] to bed, came forth again, and then fell to banqueting with Donwald and his wife . . . Whereat they sat up so long, till they had charged their stomachs with such full gorges that their heads were no sooner got to the pillow, but asleep they were — so fast that a man might have removed the chamber over them, sooner than to have waked them out of their drunken sleep.

[Donwald persuaded some of his servants to murder the king and carry his body out of the castle.]

Donwald, about the time that the murder was doing, got him amongst them that kept the watch, and so continued to company with them all the residue of the night. But in the morning when the noise was raised in the king's chamber of how the king was slain . . . he with the watch ran thither, as though he had known nothing of the matter, and breaking into the chamber, and finding cakes of blood in the bed, and on the floor about the sides of it, he forthwith slew the chamberlains as guilty of that heinous murder . . .

Finally, such was his over earnest diligence in the severe inquisition and trial of the offenders herein, that some of the lords began to mislike the matter, and to smell forth shrewd tokens, that he should not be altogether clear himself . . .

For the space of six months together, after this heinous murder thus committed, there appeared no sun by day, nor moon by night in any part of the realm, but still was the sky covered in continual clouds, and sometimes such outrageous winds arose, with lightnings and tempests, that the people were in great fear of present destruction . . .

Monstrous sights also that were seen in the Scottish kingdom that year were these: horses in Lothian, being of singular beauty and swiftness, did eat their own flesh . . . there was also a sparhawk strangled by an owl . . .

Classwork and Examinations

The works of Shakespeare are studied all over the world, and this classroom edition is being used in many different countries. Teaching methods vary from school to school and there are many different ways of examining a student's work. Some teachers and examiners expect detailed knowledge of Shakespeare's text; others ask for imaginative involvement with his characters and their situations; and there are some teachers who want their students to share in the theatrical experience of directing and performing a play. Most people use a variety of methods. This section of the book offers a few suggestions for approaches to *Macbeth* which could be used in schools and colleges to help with students' understanding and *enjoyment* of the play.

A   Discussion
B   Character Study
C   Activities
D   Context Questions
E   Comprehension Questions
F   Essays
G   Projects

A   Discussion

Talking about the play — about the issues it raises and the characters who are involved — is one of the most rewarding and pleasurable aspects of the study of Shakespeare. It makes sense to discuss each scene as it is read, sharing impressions — and perhaps correcting misapprehensions. It can be useful to compare aspects of this play with other fictions — plays, novels, films — or with modern life.

Suggestions

A1   The play opens with three witches. How would you present this scene so that a modern audience is properly impressed?

A2   Speaking of her husband, Lady Macbeth says:

> Thou would'st be great,
> Art not without ambition, but without
> The illness should attend it;
>
> *1*, 5, 17–19

What do you think she means by this? Is it not possible to be ambitious — and successful — without some kind of 'illness'?

A3   When he welcomes the King to his castle, Macbeth describes what he believes to be the duty of a loyal subject:

> . . . our duties
> Are to your throne and state, children and servants
> Which do but what they should, by doing every-
>   thing
> Safe toward your love and honour.
>
> *1*, 4, 24–5

How would *you* describe the duty of a subject, or citizen, today?

A4   At the banquet in *Act 3*, Scene 4, Macbeth sees the ghost of the murdered Banquo. How would you present this scene?

A5   Is the Porter's scene really necessary?

A6   Do these witches in fact have any power?

A7   In order to test Macduff, Malcolm describes himself as the complete opposite of an ideal king (*4*, 3, 50–102). What in your view are the qualities that would make a good ruler?

A8   What is your idea of a tyrant?

A9   Does the 'sleepwalking' scene (*Act 5*, Scene 1) cause you to feel sorry for Lady Macbeth?

A10   Is Macbeth a hero or a villain?

B   Character Study

Shakespeare is famous for his creation of characters who seem like real people. We can judge their actions, and we can try to understand their thoughts and feelings — just as we criticize and try to understand the people we know. As the play progresses, we learn to like or dislike, love or hate, them — just as though they lived in *our* world.

Characters can be studied *from the outside*, by observing what they do, and listening sensitively to what they say. This is the scholar's method: the scholar — or any reader — has access to the whole play, and can see the function of every character within the whole scheme of that play.

Another approach works *from the inside*, taking a single character and looking at the action and at the other characters from his/her point of view. This is an actor's technique in creating a character — who can have only a partial view of what is going on — for performance; and it asks for a student's inventive, sympathetic imagination. The two methods — both useful in different ways — are really complementary to each other.

Suggestions

a) from 'outside' the character

B1 What is your impression of Macbeth after reading *Act 1*, Scene 2? How is this first impression modified as the play progresses?

B2 Describe the character of Lady Macbeth before the murder of Duncan. Is she more or less guilty than her husband?

B3 Compare the character of Shakespeare's Duncan with that of Holinshed's King of Scotland. Why do you think that Shakespeare made such changes to the character?

B4 Can you suggest any reason for the presence of the Third Murderer?

B5 Do you find Macduff a sympathetic character?

b) from 'inside' the character

B6 Macbeth wrote to tell his wife about the meeting with the witches. Write a letter from Banquo to his wife, describing the same encounter.

B7 As one of the Lords attending the King, write to your wife and describe your arrival at the castle of Macbeth, and the welcome with which you were received.

B8 The Porter was present when the murder of Duncan was revealed. How would he describe the scene to his pals in the pub?

B9 What are the thoughts that pass through Macbeth's mind as he waits for his crime to be revealed? Write a 'stream-of-consciousness' account of the second part — lines 50ff — of *Act 2*, Scene 3.

B10   After the murder is discovered, both Malcolm and Donalbain flee from Scotland to ask for political asylum in (respectively) England and Ireland. How would they explain their need for refuge?

B11   In the character of one of those present at Macbeth's great feast — a Lord, Lady or Servant — tell your friends all about it.

B12   Lady Macbeth has no one to talk to — perhaps she confides in her diary? Write the entry describing her husband's strange behaviour, and her own attempts to 'cover up' for him, at the banquet in *Act 3*, Scene 4.

B13   Suppose Lady Macduff had time to write a letter, either to her husband or to a friend, before she was interrupted by the murderers in *Act 4*, Scene 2. How would she write of her love and loyalty for her husband, and her fears for herself and her children?

B14   'A remarkable case of somnambulism': Lady Macbeth's Doctor writes the case history for a medical journal.

B15   In *Act 5*, Scene 3, both the Servant and the Doctor are terrified. In the character of either, describe the situation to your friends/colleagues — or to newspaper/TV reporters.

B16   Write Macbeth's memoirs (discovered after his death) describing the last days in Dunsinane.

C   Activities

These can involve two or more students, preferably working away from the desk or study-table and using gesture and position ('body-language') as well as speech. They can help students to develop a sense of drama and the dramatic aspects of Shakespeare's play — which was written to be *performed*, not studied in a classroom.

Suggestions

C1   Act the play, or at least part of it. You don't need scenery or properties — just space and people.

C2   Speak the soliloquies of Macbeth *in your own words*.

C3   'We will speak further' (*1*, 5, 70). Plan a scene between Macbeth and Lady Macbeth before the King's visit to their castle.

C4   Macbeth twice says that, when he has more time, he would like to talk to Banquo about the witches: 'let us speak Our free hearts each to other' (*1*, 3, 154–5); *and*: 'when we can entreat an hour to serve, We would spend it in some words upon that business' (*2*, 1, 22–3). Devise two such scenes, showing how the relationship of the two men has changed between the first and second of the scenes.

C5   Give full TV coverage for the murder of Duncan — don't forget to interview the Porter and the Old Man, and to check the weather reports for that night. If possible, arrange that there should be signing for deaf people.

C6   Critics think that *Act 3*, Scene 5 was not written by Shakespeare; replace it with a new scene for the witches.

C7   Young Siward dies fighting for his country's freedom. Interview his father on a TV programme called 'Alas, poor country' (*4*, 3, 164).

C8   Bring the witches to court, and have them tried by a jury.

D   Context Questions

In written examinations, these questions present you with short passages from the play, and ask you to explain them. They are intended to test your knowledge of the play and your understanding of its words. Usually you have to make a choice of passages: there may be five on the paper, and you are asked to choose three. Be very sure that you know exactly how many passages you must choose. Study the ones offered to you, and select those you feel most certain of. Make your answers accurate and concise — don't waste time writing more than the examiner is asking for.

D1   Do not muse at me, my most worthy friends;
I have a strange infirmity, which is nothing
To those that know me. Come, love and health
   to all:
Then, I'll sit down. Give me some wine, fill full;
I drink to the general joy of the whole table.

   (i)   Who is speaking, and on what occasion?
   (ii) What has caused him to behave strangely?
   (iii) What happens immediately after these lines?

D2   Art thou afeard
To be the same in thine own act and valour
As thou art in desire? Wouldst thou have that
Which thou esteem'st the ornament of life,
And live a coward in thine own esteem?

(i)   Who is speaking, and to whom?
(ii) What is the person addressed afraid to do?
(iii) What effect does this speech have on the person
      addressed?

D3 Wisdom! to leave his wife, to leave his babes,
His mansion and his titles, in a place
From whence himself does fly? He loves us not,
He wants the natural touch.

(i)   Who is speaking, and to whom?
(ii) What person is being spoken about?
(iii) What happens to the speaker shortly after these lines
      have been spoken?

D4 A heavy summons lies like lead upon me,
And yet I would not sleep: merciful powers!
Restrain in me the cursed thoughts that nature
Gives way to in repose. Give me my sword!

(i)   Who is the speaker? Who accompanies him?
(ii) Why is he unwilling to sleep?
(iii) Why does he ask for his sword?

D5 Have you considered of my speeches? Know
That it was he, in the times past, which held you
So under fortune, which you thought had been
Our innocent self.

(i)   Who is speaking? To whom does he speak?
(ii) Who is the 'he' referred to?
(iii) What does the speaker want his hearers to do?

D6   did he not straight,
In pious rage the two delinquents tear,
That were the slaves of drink, and thralls of sleep?
Was not that nobly done? Ay, and wisely, too;
For 'twould have anger'd any heart alive
To hear the men deny't.

    (i) Who is speaking, and about whom?
    (ii) Who are the 'two delinquents'?
    (iii) What would they have denied?

D7 That which hath made them drunk hath made me
       bold,
  What hath quench'd them hath given me fire. Hark!
  Peace!
  It was the owl that shriek'd, the fatal bellman
  Which gives the stern'st good-night. He is about it.

    (i) Who is speaking?
    (ii) What is the speaker listening for?
    (iii) Who comes on to the stage after these lines? What has he
        done?

D8 We hear our bloody cousins are bestow'd
  In England and in Ireland, not confessing
  Their cruel parricide, filling their hearers
  With strange invention. But of that tomorrow,
  When, therewithal, we shall have cause of state
  Craving us jointly.

    (i) Who is speaking, and to whom does he speak?
    (ii) Who are the 'bloody cousins'?
    (iii) Will the person addressed attend the meeting tomorrow?
        Why?

E   Comprehension Questions

These also present passages from the play and ask questions about
them, and again you often have a choice of passages. But the
extracts are much longer than those presented as context questions.
A detailed knowledge of the language of the play is asked for here,
and you must be able to express unusual or archaic phrases in your
own words; you may also be asked to comment critically on the
effectiveness of Shakespeare's language.

E1 *Lady Macbeth*

           What beast was't, then,
That made you break this enterprise to me?
When you durst do it, then you were a man;

And, to be more than what you were, you would
Be so much more the man. Nor time nor place   5
Did then adhere, and yet you would make both:
They have made themselves, and that their fitness
  now
Does unmake you. I have given suck, and know
How tender 'tis to love the babe that milks me:
I would, while it was smiling in my face,   10
Have pluck'd my nipple from his boneless gums,
And dash'd the brains out, had I so sworn as you
Have done to this.

    (i) Give the precise location of this speech, explaining its
       cause and effect.
   (ii) What is the meaning of 'break this enterprise to me'
       (line 2); 'Nor time nor place Did then adhere' (lines
       5–6); 'I have given suck' (line 8); 'dash'd the brains out'
       (line 12)?
  (iii) What does this speech tell you about Lady Macbeth?
  (iv) What effect do these lines have on Macbeth?

E2   *Malcolm*

          Macduff, this noble passion,
Child of integrity, hath from my soul
Wip'd the black scruples, reconcil'd my thoughts
To thy good truth and honour. Devilish Macbeth
By many of these trains hath sought to win me   5
Into his power, and modest wisdom plucks me
From over-credulous haste; but God above
Deal between me and thee! for even now
I put myself to thy direction, and
Unspeak mine own detraction, here abjure   10
The taints and blames I laid upon myself,
For strangers to my nature. I am yet
Unknown to woman; never was forsworn;
Scarcely have coveted what was mine own;
At no time broke my faith; would not betray   15
The devil to his fellow; and delight
No less in truth than life; my first false speaking
Was this upon myself.

    (i) Explain what is meant by 'reconcil'd my thoughts'
       (line 3); 'trains' (line 5); 'over-credulous haste' (line 7);

'put myself to thy direction' (line 9); 'Unknown to woman' (line 13).

(ii) Describe one of the 'taints and blames' (line 11) which Malcolm accused himself of possessing.

(iii) Which of these 'taints and blames' did Macduff think the most serious?

(iv) How does the language of this passage convince you of Malcolm's seriousness?

E3 *Macbeth*

> To be thus is nothing;
> But to be safely thus. Our fears in Banquo
> Stick deep, and in his royalty of nature
> Reigns that which would be fear'd: 'tis much he dares,
> And, to that dauntless temper of his mind,   5
> He hath a wisdom that doth guide his valour
> To act in safety. There is none but he
> Whose being I do fear; and under him
> My genius is rebuk'd, as, it is said,
> Mark Antony's was by Caesar. He chid the sisters   10
> When first they put the name of king upon me,
> And bade them speak to him; then, prophet-like,
> They hail'd him father to a line of kings.
> Upon my head they plac'd a fruitless crown,
> And put a barren sceptre in my gripe,   15
> Thence to be wrench'd with an unlineal hand,
> No son of mine succeeding. If't be so,
> For Banquo's issue have I fil'd my mind;
> For them the gracious Duncan have I murder'd;
> Put rancours in the vessel of my peace   20
> Only for them; and mine eternal jewel
> Given to the common enemy of man,
> To make them kings, the seed of Banquo kings!

(i) What does Macbeth mean when he says 'To be thus is nothing; But to be safely thus' (lines 1–2)?

(ii) Give the precise meaning of 'put the name of king upon me' (line 11), 'an unlineal hand' (line 16), 'mine eternal jewel' (line 21); 'the common enemy of man' (line 22), 'seed' (line 23).

(iii) Comment on the language of lines 14–17 ('Upon my head . . . no son of mine succeeding.')

(iv) Express in your own words the thoughts of lines 17–23 ('For Banquo's issue . . . the seed of Banquo kings').

F   Essays

These will usually give you a specific topic to discuss, or perhaps a question that must be answered, in writing, *with a reasoned argument*. They *never* want you to tell the story of the play — so don't! Your examiner — or teacher — has read the play, and does not need to be reminded of it. Relevant quotations will always help you to make your points more strongly.

F1   How important is the influence of Lady Macbeth on her husband?

F2   What have you learned from *Macbeth* about the Elizabethan concept of the king?

F3   Describe the character of Macduff, and show how Shakespeare wins respect and approval for him.

F4   Give an account of the part played by the supernatural in *Macbeth*.

F5   We will establish our estate upon
              Our eldest, Malcolm.

Explain why this is an important announcement.

F6   Compare and contrast Lady Macbeth and Lady Macduff.

F7   What means does Shakespeare use to create 'atmosphere' in *Macbeth*?

F8   At the beginning of the play Macbeth writes to his wife as 'my dearest partner of greatness'. How does their relationship change during the play?

F9   Give an account of the function of Ross in the play.

F10   Describe how Duncan rewards good and bad service.

F11   Discuss the importance of sleep in *Macbeth*.

F12   Is there any comedy in *Macbeth*? Is it necessary?

F13   'Everyone in the play either suspects, or is himself suspected.' Show how true this is.

F14 Do you feel any pity for Macbeth's 'fiend-like queen'?

G Projects

In some schools, students are asked to do more 'free-ranging' work, which takes them outside the text — but which should always be relevant to the play. Such Projects may demand skills other than reading and writing: design and artwork, for instance, may be involved. Sometimes a 'portfolio' of work is assembled over a considerable period of time; and this can be presented to the examiner as part of the student's work for assessment.

The availability of resources will, obviously, do much to determine the nature of the Projects; but this is something that only the local teachers will understand. However, there is always help to be found in libraries, museums, and art galleries.

Suggestions

G1 Witches and witchcraft.

G2 Sleep.

G3 Consorts.

G4 Scotland.

G5 The Sources of *Macbeth*.

G6 Great Actors and Actresses in *Macbeth*.

Background

England c. 1606

When Shakespeare was writing *Macbeth*, most people believed that the sun went round the earth. They were taught that this was a divinely ordered scheme of things, and that — in England — God had instituted a Church and ordained a Monarchy for the right government of the land and the populace.

'The past is a foreign country; they do things differently there.'

L.P. Hartley

Government

For most of Shakespeare's life, the reigning monarch of England was Queen Elizabeth I; when she died, she was succeeded by King James I. He was also King of Scotland (James VI), and the two kingdoms were united in 1603 by his accession to the English throne. With his counsellors and ministers, James governed the nation (population less than six million) from London, although not more than half a million people inhabited the capital city. In the rest of the country, law and order were maintained by the land-owners and enforced by their deputies. The average man had no vote — and his wife had no rights at all.

Religion

At this time, England was a Christian country. All children were baptized, soon after they were born, into the Church of England; they were taught the essentials of the Christian faith, and instructed in their duty to God and to humankind.

Marriages were performed, and funerals conducted, only by the licensed clergy and in accordance with the Church's rites and ceremonies. Attendance at divine service was compulsory; absences (without good — medical — reason) could be punished by fines. By such means, the authorities were able to keep some check on the populace — recording births, marriages, and deaths; being alert to any religious nonconformity, which could be politically dangerous; and ensuring a minimum of orthodox instruction through the official 'Homilies' which were regularly preached from the pulpits of all parish churches throughout the realm.

Following Henry VIII's break away from the Church of Rome, all people in England were able to hear the church services *in their own language*. The Book of Common Prayer was used in every church, and an English translation of the Bible was read aloud in public. The Christian religion had never been so well taught before!

Education

School education reinforced the Church's teaching. From the age of four, boys might attend the 'petty school' (French *'petite école'*) to learn the rudiments of reading and writing along with a few prayers; some schools also included work with numbers. At the age of seven, the boy was ready for the grammar school (if his father was willing and able to pay the fees). Here, a thorough grounding in Latin grammar was followed by translation work and the study of Roman authors, paying attention as much to style as to matter. The arts of fine writing were thus inculcated from early youth.

A very few students proceeded to university; these were either clever scholarship boys, or else the sons of noblemen. Girls stayed at home, and acquired domestic and social skills — cooking, sewing, perhaps even music. The lucky ones might learn to read and write.

Language

At the start of the sixteenth century the English had a very poor opinion of their own language: there was little serious writing in English, and hardly any literature. Latin was the language of international scholarship, and Englishmen admired the eloquence of the Romans. They made many translations, and in this way they extended the resources of their own language, increasing its vocabulary and stretching its grammatical structures. French, Italian, and Spanish works were also translated, and — for the first time — there were English versions of the Bible.

By the end of the century, English was a language to be proud of: it was rich in synonyms, capable of infinite variety and subtlety, and ready for all kinds of word-play — especially the *puns*, for which Shakespeare's English is renowned.

Drama

The great art-form of the Elizabethan and Jacobean age was its drama. The Elizabethans inherited a tradition of play-acting from the Middle Ages, and they reinforced this by reading and translating the Roman playwrights. At the beginning of the sixteenth century, plays were performed by groups of actors, all-male companies (boys acted the female roles) who travelled from town to town, setting up their stages in open places (such as inn-yards) or, with the permission of the owner, in the hall of some noble house. The touring companies continued, in the provinces, into the seventeenth century; but in London, in 1576, a new building was erected for the performance of plays. This was the Theatre, the first purpose-built playhouse in England. Other playhouses followed, (including Shakespeare's own theatre, the Globe) and the English drama reached new heights of eloquence.

There were those who disapproved, of course. The theatres, which brought large crowds together, could encourage the spread of disease — and dangerous ideas. During the summer, when the plague was at its worst, the playhouses were closed. A constant censorship was imposed, more or less severe at different times. The Puritan faction tried to close down the theatres, but — partly because there was royal favour for the drama, and partly because the buildings were outside the city limits — they did not succeed until 1642.

Theatre

From contemporary comments and sketches — most particularly a drawing by a Dutch visitor, Johannes de Witt — it is possible to form some idea of the typical Elizabethan playhouse for which most of Shakespeare's plays were written. Hexagonal in shape, it had three roofed galleries encircling an open courtyard. The plain, high stage projected into the yard, where it was surrounded by the audience of standing 'groundlings'. At the back were two doors for the actors' entrances and exits; and above these doors was a balcony — useful for a musicians' gallery or for the acting of scenes *above*. Over the stage was a thatched roof, supported on two pillars, forming a canopy — which seems to have been painted with the sun, moon and stars for the 'heavens'.

Underneath was space (concealed by curtaining) which could be used by characters ascending and descending through a trap-door in the stage. Costumes and properties were kept backstage, in the 'tiring house'. The actors dressed lavishly, often wearing the secondhand clothes bestowed by rich patrons. Stage properties were important for defining a location, but the dramatist's own words were needed to explain the time of day, since all performances took place in the early afternoon.

Selected Further Reading

Source

Bullough, Geoffrey, *The Narrative and Dramatic Sources of Shakespeare*, vol. VII (London, 1973).

Muir, Kenneth, *The Sources of Shakespeare's Plays*, (London, 1977).

Criticism

There are useful chapters, or essays, on *Macbeth* in the following books:

Bayley, John, *Shakespeare and Tragedy*, (London, 1981).

Bradley, A.C., *Shakespearean Tragedy*, (London, 1904; reprinted 1978).

Brown, J.R. (ed.), *Focus on 'Macbeth'*, (London, 1982).

Campbell, Lily B., *Shakespeare's Tragic Heroes*, (Cambridge, 1930).

Coleridge, S.T., *Coleridge's Criticism of Shakespeare*, (c. 1808; ed. R.A. Foakes, London, 1989).

Holloway, John, *The Story of the Night*, (London, 1961).

Honigmann, E.A.J., *Shakespeare, Seven Tragedies*, (London, 1976).

Knight, G. Wilson, *The Imperial Theme*, (London, 1931). *The Wheel of Fire*, (London, 1930).

Knights, L.C., *Explorations*, (Cambridge, 1933). *Some Shakespearean Themes*, (London, 1959).

Spurgeon, Caroline, *Shakespeare's Imagery*, (Cambridge, 1935).

Stewart, J.I.M., *Character and Motive in Shakespeare*, (London, 1949).

Background

Blake, N.F., *Shakespeare's Language: an Introduction*, (Methuen, 1983).

Muir, K., and Schoenbaum, S., *A New Companion to Shakespeare Studies*, (Cambridge, 1971).

Schoenbaum, S., *William Shakespeare: A Documentary Life*, (Oxford, 1975).

Thomson, Peter, *Shakespeare's Theatre*, (Routledge and Kegan Paul, 1983).

William Shakespeare, 1564–1616

Elizabeth I was Queen of England when Shakespeare was born in 1564. He was the son of a tradesman who made and sold gloves in the small town of Stratford-upon-Avon, and he was educated at the grammar school in that town. Shakespeare did not go to university when he left school, but worked, perhaps, in his father's business. When he was eighteen he married Anne Hathaway, who became the mother of his daughter, Susanna, in 1583, and of twins in 1585.

There is nothing exciting, or even unusual, in this story; and from 1585 until 1592 there are no documents that can tell us anything at all about Shakespeare. But we have learned that in 1592 he was known in London, and that he had become both an actor and a playwright.

We do not know when Shakespeare wrote his first play, and indeed we are not sure of the order in which he wrote his works. If you look on page 111 at the list of his writings and their approximate dates, you will see how he started by writing plays on subjects taken from the history of England. No doubt this was partly because he was always an intensely patriotic man—but he was also a very shrewd business-man. He could see that the theatre audiences enjoyed being shown their own history, and it was certain that he would make a profit from this kind of drama.

The plays in the next group are mainly comedies, with romantic love stories of young people who fall in love with one another, and at the end of the play marry and live happily ever after.

At the end of the sixteenth century the happiness disappears, and Shakespeare's plays become melancholy, bitter, and tragic. This change may have been caused by some sadness in the writer's life (one of his twins died in 1596). Shakespeare, however, was not the only writer whose works at this time were very serious. The whole of England was facing a crisis. Queen Elizabeth I was growing old. She was greatly loved, and the people were sad to think she must soon die; they were also afraid, for the Queen had never married, and so there was no child to succeed her.

When James I came to the throne in 1603, Shakespeare continued to write serious drama—the great tragedies and the plays based on Roman history (such as *Julius Caesar*) for which he is most famous. Finally, before he retired from the theatre, he wrote another set of comedies. These all have the same theme: they tell of happiness which is lost, and then found again.

Shakespeare returned from London to Stratford, his home town. He was rich and successful, and he owned one of the biggest houses in the town. He died in 1616.

Shakespeare also wrote two long poems, and a collection of sonnets. The sonnets describe two love-affairs, but we do not know who the lovers were. Although there are many public documents concerned with his career as a writer and a business-man, Shakespeare has hidden his personal life from us. A nineteenth-century poet, Matthew Arnold, addressed Shakespeare in a poem, and wrote 'We ask and ask—Thou smilest, and art still'.

There is not even a trustworthy portrait of the world's greatest dramatist.

Approximate order of composition of Shakespeare's works

Period	Comedies	History plays	Tragedies	Poems
I	Comedy of Errors	Henry VI, part 1	Titus Andronicus	
	Taming of the Shrew	Henry VI, part 2		
1594	Two Gentlemen of Verona	Henry VI, part 3		Venus and Adonis
		Richard III		Rape of Lucrece
	Love's Labour's Lost	King John		
II	Midsummer Night's Dream	Richard II	Romeo and Juliet	Sonnets
	Merchant of Venice	Henry IV, part 1		
1599	Merry Wives of Windsor	Henry IV, part 2		
	Much Ado About Nothing			
	As You Like It	Henry V		
III	Twelfth Night		Julius Caesar	
	Troilus and Cressida		Hamlet	
1608	Measure for Measure		Othello	
	All's Well That Ends Well		Timon of Athens	
			King Lear	
			Macbeth	
			Antony and Cleopatra	
			Coriolanus	
IV	Pericles			
	Cymbeline			
1613	The Winter's Tale	Henry VIII		
	The Tempest			